50 Shades of Stitches

Classic and Contemporary Knitting Patterns

with Step-by-Step Instructions

Copyright © 2019 by SCR Media Inc. All rights reserved. This book or any portion thereof cannot be reproduced or used in any manner whatsoever without the express written permission of the publisher.

Printed in the United States of America First Printing, 2019

ISBN 978-1-63227-2676

SCR MEDIA Inc. Box 7103
Delray Beach Fl. 33482
561-909-6975

If you like this book and found some benefit in reading it, I'd like to hear from you and hope that you could take some time to post a review on Amazon. Your feedback and support will help the author to greatly improve her writing craft for future projects and make this book even better. Just type this link into your web browser **Getbook.at/Vol2** *or scan QR code*

Contents

Pattern 1 1

Pattern 2 3

Pattern 3 6

Pattern 4 9

Pattern 5 11

Pattern 6 13

Pattern 7 15

Pattern 8 17

Pattern 9 19

Pattern 10 21

Pattern 11 23

Pattern 12 25

Pattern 13 28

Pattern 14 31

Pattern 15 34

Pattern 16 36

Pattern 17 38

Pattern 18 40

Pattern 19 42

Pattern 20 44

Pattern 21 46

Pattern 22 48

Pattern 23 50

Pattern 24 52

Pattern 25 54
Pattern 26 56
Pattern 27 58
Pattern 28 60
Pattern 29 62
Pattern 30 64
Pattern 31 66
Pattern 32 68
Pattern 33 70
Pattern 34 72
Pattern 35 74
Pattern 36 77
Pattern 37 79
Pattern 38 81
Pattern 39 83
Pattern 40 85
Pattern 41 87
Pattern 42 90
Pattern 43 92
Pattern 44 94
Pattern 45 97
Pattern 46 99
Pattern 47 101
Pattern 48 103
Pattern 49 105
Pattern 50 109

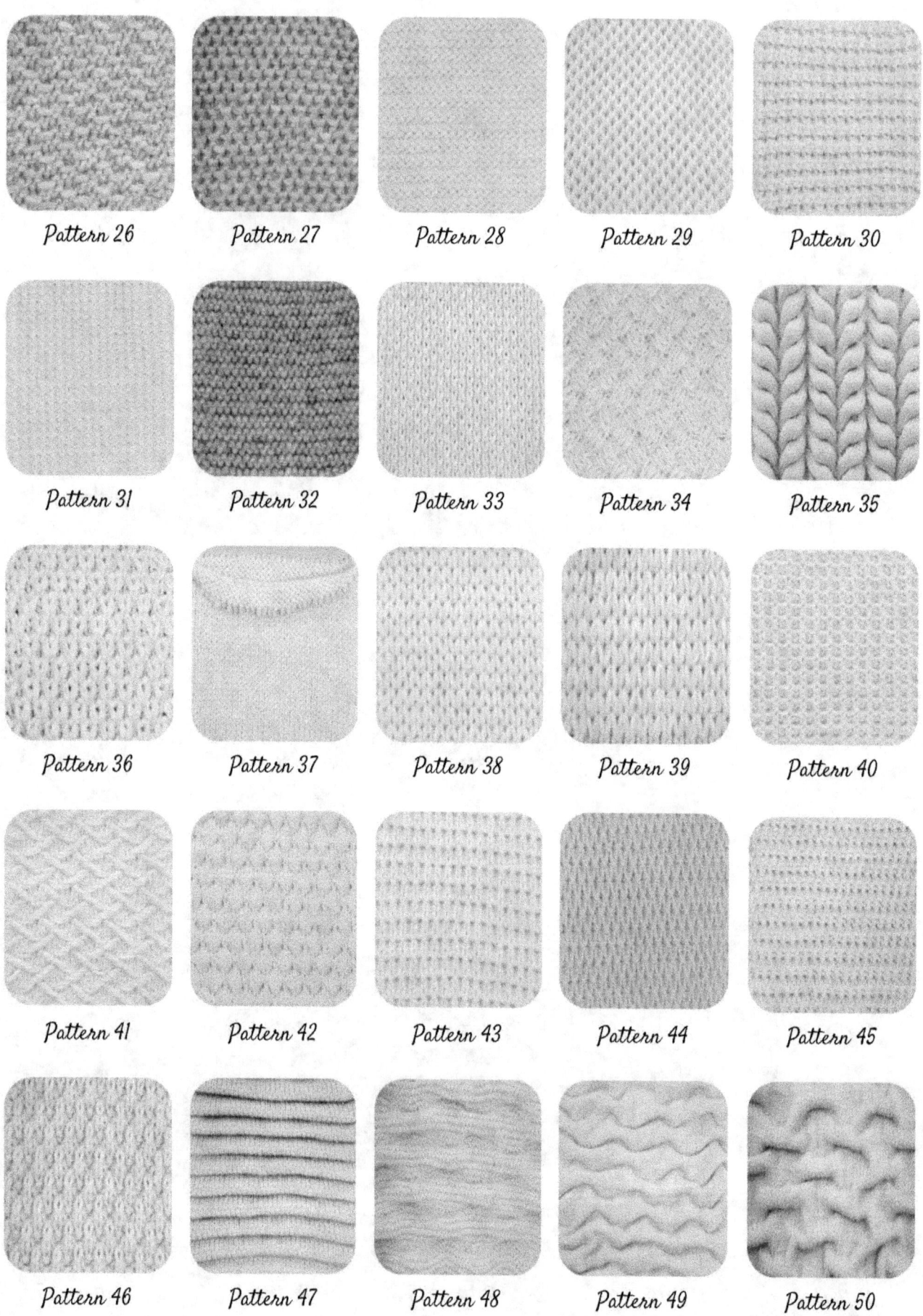

Introduction

This book offers classic and contemporary patterns that reflect modern trends of knitting. It includes popular timeless patterns and ideas of transforming classic into trendy designs.

Hand knitting is unique, and even top designers use it. But designers' creations never look like homemade knits. Their handmade knits are always impeccably crafted. How do they achieve high craftsmanship? And how can we improve our knitting skills?

Impeccable execution comes with experience. There is also a certain level of taste, vision, and professionalism, including selecting yarns and knitting patterns. Designers know that simple knitwear designs may require catchy knitting patterns or yarns.

Choosing the right size of needles for a particular yarn or a knitting pattern is also essential for flawless execution since it affects knitting quality. The same pattern can come out too loose or too tight, or simply different, depending on the needles' size.

Stitches can be knitted through the front leg or the back leg, and, in each method of knitting, the purl stitch must be worked differently. Depending on how the purl stitch is worked, it sets up the knit stitch to be knitted either through the front leg or through the back leg; therefore, the knit and purl stitches must correspond to a particular way of knitting. The right choice of the method of knitting for a specific pattern, i.e., through the front leg or the back leg, and working the purl stitches correctly, affect the knit fabric's evenness and quality.

And don't forget about yarn tension. In order to knit evenly, the yarn tension must always be the same, the working yarn must be held tightly and controlled by the index finger, and stitches must be worked on the tips of the needles. Until this process becomes automatic, the yarn tension must be controlled.

Like any other craft, hand knitting requires practice. The more you knit, the better and faster you knit. Knit more! It's fun, functional, and fashionable. With practice, you can improve your skills, so your hand knits will be impeccable.

— Marina Molo

Recommendations

Two Methods of Knitting Stitches

Knitting through the front legs: knit through the front leg, inserting the right needle through the stitch from left to right; work the purl stitch as follows: with the working yarn in front of the stitch, insert the right needle through the stitch from back to front and wrap the working yarn forward (i.e., from yourself) around the tip of the right needle, then pull it with the needle through the stitch. The purl stitch that is worked this way sets up the knit stitch to be knitted through the front leg.

Knitting through the back legs: knit through the back leg, inserting the right needle through the stitch from right to left; work the purl stitch as follows: with the working yarn in front of the stitch, insert the right needle through the stitch from back to front, move the working yarn under the right needle, and pull it with the needle through the stitch. The purl stitch that is worked this way sets up the knit stitch to be knitted through the back leg.

How to Do Yarn Over

Unless indicated otherwise, the working yarn goes from the needle's front towards the back when the knit stitch follows yarn over. In this case, the description reads "yarn over forward (i.e., from yourself)." When the purl stitch follows yarn over, the working yarn goes from behind the needle towards the front. In this case, the description reads "yarn over backward (i.e., to yourself). "

How to Work Edge Stitches

The first way: Slip the first edge stitch; purl the last edge stitch as if to purl in knitting through back leg as follows: with the working yarn in front of the stitch, insert the right needle through the stitch from back to front, then move the working yarn under the right needle and pull it with the needle through the stitch. Note: Regardless of the method of knitting, through the front legs or the back legs, purl the last edge stitch as if to purl in knitting through the back leg, as this way of working the last edge stitch creates more tight and even edges.

The second way: Knit both the first edge stitch and the last edge stitch through the front leg (or, depending on the pattern, through the back legs). Note: This way of working the edge stitches is used in patterns in which otherwise the left edge comes out loose and slightly stretchy. This way of knitting the edge stitches creates even edges on both sides.

Three Methods of Binding off Stitches

The first method: *knit 2 together through the back legs (or purl 2 together as if to purl in knitting through the back legs for binding off purlwise), then slip the received stitch from the right needle to the left one* repeat from

* to * until the end of the row.

The second method: slip the edge stitch onto the right needle, knit 1 (or purl 1 as if to purl in knitting through the back leg for binding off purlwise), then pass the edge stitch over the knitted (or purled) stitch; *now there is 1 stitch on the right needle; knit (or purl) the next stitch; now there are 2 stitches on the right needle; insert the left needle through the 1st stitch from left to right and pass it over the 2nd stitch* repeat from * to * until the end of the row.

Note: The second method of binding off creates the edge tighter than the first method does. For a tighter edge, bind off using thinner needles than the working ones.

The third method: Unless indicated otherwise, after knitting the last row on the Front Side, turn your work over; the Back Side: slip all stitches from the left needle to the right one; as a result, the working yarn is at the end of the row; turn your work over; the Front Side: slip 2 stitches from the left needle to the right one; insert the left needle through the 1st slipped stitch from left to right and pass it over the 2nd one; now there is 1 stitch on the right needle; *slip 1 stitch from the left needle to the right one; insert the left needle through the 1st stitch on the right needle from left to right and pass it over the 2nd one; now there is 1 stitch on the right needle* repeat from * to * until the end of the row.

Note: This method is more appropriate for binding off ribbed stitches, braids, cables, ruffles, and loosely knitted patterns, as it prevents the edge from stretching, creating a tight chain of small stitches, which, in many cases, does not require finishing. For trimming this edge, bind off loosely, using larger needles than the working ones to create larger edge stitches.

How to Count Rows

Count the edge stitches instead of rows; counting the actual rows, especially in complicated patterns, can be difficult or impossible. Each edge stitch is equal to 2 rows. Count the edge stitches' chain as follows: 2, 4, 6, 8, 10, etc. It's fast and easy.

Pattern 1

Cast on a multiple of 10, plus 2 edge stitches. Ten-stitch repeat. Repeat rows: 1-8. The edge stitches are not included in the description below and must be added. Slip the first edge stitch; purl the last edge stitch as if to

purl in knitting through the back leg as follows: insert the right needle through the stitch from back to front, move the working yarn under the right needle, and pull it with the needle through the stitch.

Description:

Row 1: Knit all the stitches.

Row 2: Knit all the stitches.

Row 3: *Knit 7—loosely—out of 1 stitch as follows: knit 1—do not release the left needle yet— yarn over forward (i.e., from yourself), knit 1, yarn over (i.e., from yourself), knit 1, yarn over forward (i.e., from yourself), knit 1, then release the left needle (now there are 7 stitches on the right needle instead of 1), repeat knitting 7 out of 1 stitch 4 more times, then knit 5* repeat from * to * until the end of the row.

Row 4: Knit all the stitches as follows: *knit 5, knit the next 7 together through the back legs, repeat knitting the next 7 together through the back legs 4 more times* repeat from * to * until the end of the row.

Row 5: Knit all the stitches.

Row 6: Knit all the stitches.

Row 7: Knit 4, *knit 7 out of 1 stitch as described in row 3, repeat 4 more times, then knit 5* repeat from * to * until the end of the row before the edge stitch, the last 6 stitches, knit 7 out of 1 stitch as described in row 3, repeat 4 more times, then knit 1.

Row 8: Knit all the stitches as follows: knit 1, *knit the next 7 together through the back legs, repeat knitting 7 together through the back legs 4 more times, then knit the next 5* repeat from * to * until the end of the row before the edge stitch, the last 9 stitches, knit 7 together through the back legs, repeat knitting 7 together through the back legs 4 more times, then knit the last 4.

Repeat rows: 1-8.

Bind off as follows: slip the edge stitch onto the right needle, knit 1, then insert the left needle through the slipped edge stitch from left to right and pass it over the knitted stitch; *now there is 1 stitch on the right needle, knit the next 1, insert the left needle through the 1st stitch from left to right and pass it over the 2nd stitch* repeat from * to * until the end of the row.

Pattern 2

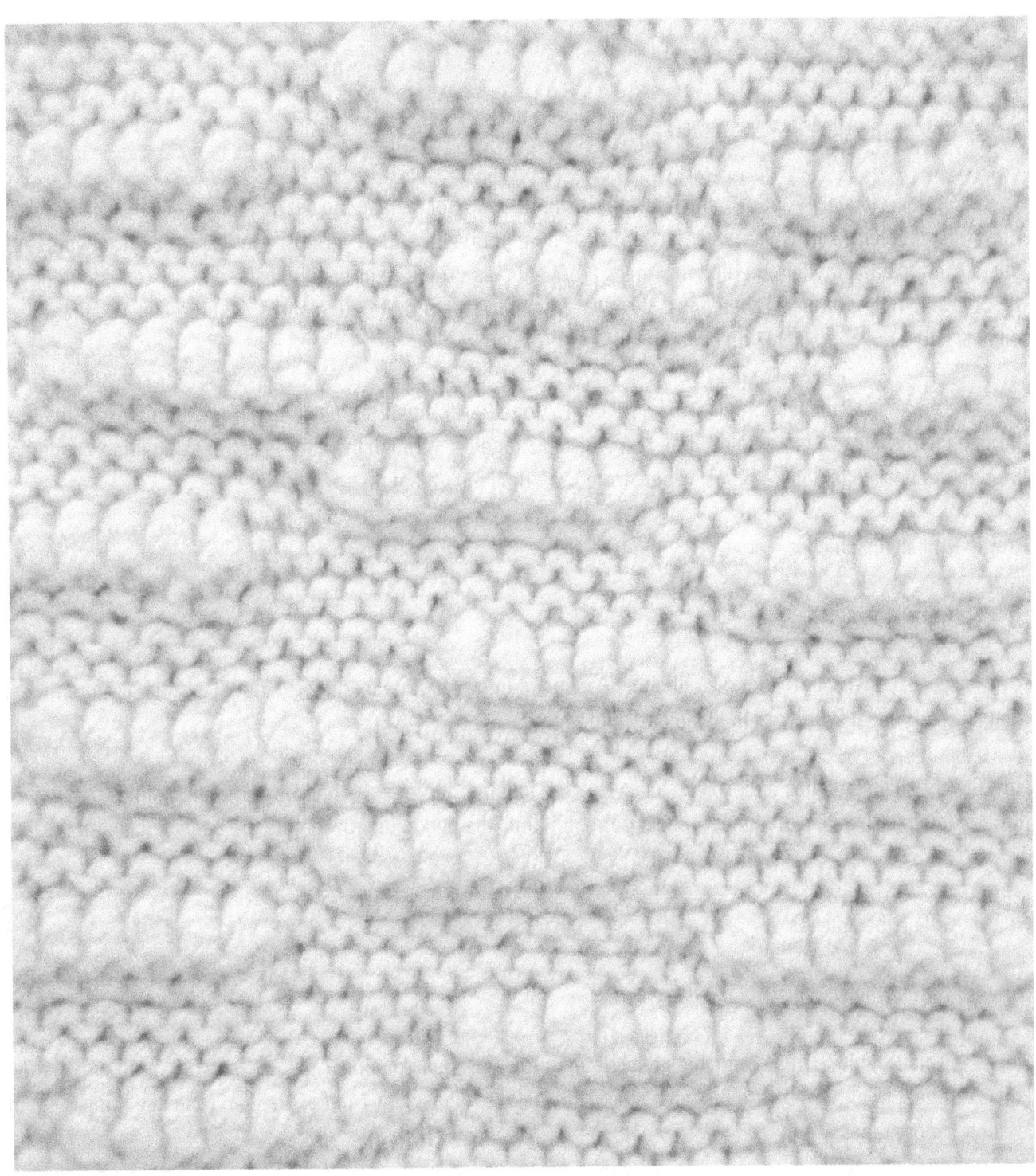

Cast on a multiple of 20, plus 10 and 2 edge stitches. Twenty-stitch repeat. Repeat rows: 1-16. The edge stitches are not included in the description below and must be added. Slip the first edge stitch; purl the last edge stitch

as if to purl in knitting through the back leg as follows: insert the right needle through the stitch from back to front, move the working yarn under the right needle, and pull it with the needle through the stitch.

Description:

Row 1: Knit all the stitches.

Row 2: Knit all the stitches.

Row 3: *Knit 7—loosely—out of 1 stitch as follows: knit 1—do not release the left needle yet— yarn over forward (i.e., from yourself), knit 1, yarn over forward (i.e., from yourself), knit 1, yarn over forward (i.e., from yourself), knit 1, then release the left needle (now there are 7 stitches on the right needle instead of 1), repeat knitting 7 out of 1 stitch 6 more times, then knit 13* repeat from * to * before the edge stitch, knit the last 10 stitches as follows: knit 7 out of 1 stitch 7 times, then knit 3.

Row 4: Knit all the stitches as follows: knit 3, knit 7 together through the back legs, repeat knitting 7 together through the back legs 6 more times, then *knit 13, knit 7 together through the back legs, repeat knitting 7 together through the back legs 6 more times* repeat from * to * until the end of the row.

Row 5: Knit all the stitches.

Row 6: Knit all the stitches.

Row 7: Knit 10, then *knit 7 out of 1 stitch as described in row 3, repeat knitting 7 out of 1 stitch 6 more times, then knit 13* repeat from * to * until the end of the row.

Row 8: Knit all the stitches as follows: *knit 13, knit 7 together through the back legs, repeat knitting 7 together through the back legs 6 more times* repeat from * to * until the end of the row before the edge stitch, knit the last 10.

Row 9: Knit all the stitches.

Row 10: Knit all the stitches.

Row 11: Knit 3, *knit 7 out of 1 stitch as described in row 3, repeat knitting 7 out of 1 stitch 6 more times, then knit 13* repeat from * to * before the edge stitch, the last 7 stitches, knit 7 out of 1 stitch, repeat knitting 7 out of 1 stitch 6 more times.

Row 12: Knit all the stitches as follows: knit 7 together through the back legs, repeat 6 times, then *knit 13, knit 7 together through the back legs, repeat knitting 7 together through the back legs 6 more times* repeat from * to * until the end of the row before the edge stitch, knit the last 3.

Row 13: Knit all the stitches.

Row 14: Knit all the stitches.

Row 15: *Knit 13, then knit 7 out of 1 stitch as described in row 3, repeat knitting 7 out of 1 stitch 6 more times* repeat from * to * before the edge stitch, knit the last 10.

Row 16: Knit all the stitches as follows: knit 10, then *knit 7 together through the back legs, repeat knitting 7 together through the back legs 5 more times, then knit 14* repeat from * to * until the end of the row.

Repeat rows: 1-16.

Bind off as follows: slip the edge stitch onto the right needle, knit 1, then insert the left needle through the slipped edge stitch from left to right and pass it over the knitted stitch; *now there is 1 stitch on the right needle, knit the next 1, insert the left needle through the 1st stitch from left to right and pass it over the 2nd stitch* repeat from * to * until the end of the row.

Pattern 3

Cast on a multiple of 20, plus 10 and 2 edge stitches. Twenty-stitch repeat. Repeat rows: 1-16. The edge stitches are not included in the description below and must be added. Slip the first edge stitch; purl the last edge stitch

as if to purl in knitting through the back leg as follows: insert the right needle through the stitch from back to front, move the working yarn under the right needle, and pull it with the needle through the stitch.

Description:

Row 1: Knit all the stitches.

Row 2: Knit all the stitches.

Row 3: *Knit 7—loosely—out of 1 stitch as follows: knit 1—do not release the left needle yet—yarn over forward (i.e., from yourself), knit 1, yarn over forward (i.e., from yourself), knit 1, yarn over forward (i.e., from yourself), knit 1, then release the left needle, repeat knitting 7 out of 1 stitch 5 more times, then knit 14* repeat from * to * the last 10 stitches, before the edge stitch, knit as follows: knit 7 out 1 stitch 6 times, then knit 4.

Row 4: Knit all the stitches as follows: knit 4, knit 7 together through the back legs, repeat knitting 7 together through the back legs 5 more times, then knit 14, then knit 7 together through the back legs 5 more times.

Row 5: Knit all the stitches.

Row 6: Knit all the stitches.

Row 7: Knit 10, *knit 7 out of 1 stitch 6 times as described in row 3, then knit 14* repeat from * to * until the end of the row.

Row 8: Knit all the stitches as follows: *knit 14, knit 7 together through the back legs, repeat knitting 7 together through the back legs 5 more times* repeat from * to * before the edge stitch, knit the last 10.

Row 9: Knit all the stitches.

Row 10: Knit all the stitches.

Row 11: Knit 4, *knit 7 out of 1 stitch as described in row 3, repeat knitting 7 out of 1 stitch 5 more times, then knit 14* repeat from * to * before the edge stitch, the last 6 stitches, knit 7 out of 1 stitch 6 times.

Row 12: Knit all the stitches as follows: knit 7 together through the back legs, repeat 5 more times, then *knit 14, knit 7 together through the back legs, repeat knitting 7 together through the back legs 5 more times* repeat from * to * before the edge stitch, knit the last 4.

Row 13: Knit all the stitches.

Row 14: Knit all the stitches.

Row 15: *Knit 14, knit 7 out of 1 stitch as described in row 3, repeat knitting 7 out of 1 stitch 5 more times* repeat from * to * before the edge stitch, knit the last 10.

Row 16: Knit all the stitches as follows: knit 10, then *knit 7 together through the back legs, repeat knitting 7 together through the back legs 5 more times, then knit 14* repeat from * to * until the end of the row.

Repeat rows: 1-16.

Bind off as follows: slip the edge stitch onto the right needle, knit 1, then insert the left needle through the slipped edge stitch from left to right and pass it over the knitted stitch; *now there is 1 stitch on the right needle, knit the next 1, insert the left needle through the 1st stitch from left to right and pass it over the 2nd stitch* repeat from * to * until the end of the row.

Pattern 4

Cast on a multiple of 2, plus 2 edge stitches. Two-stitch repeat. Repeat rows: 2-7. The edge stitches are not included in the description below and must be added. Slip the first edge stitch; purl the last edge stitch as if to

purl in knitting through the back leg as follows: insert the right needle through the stitch from back to front, move the working yarn under the right needle, and pull it with the needle through the stitch.

Knit through the front leg; purl as follows: with the working yarn in front of the stitch, wrap the working yarn forward (i.e., from yourself) around the tip of the right needle, then pull the yarn with the needle through the stitch. The purl stitch that is worked this way sets up the knit stitch to be knitted through the front leg.

Description:

Row 1 (set up row): *Knit 1, purl 1* repeat from * to * until the end of the row.

Row 2: *Yarn over forward (i.e., from yourself), slip 1 purlwise, purl 1* repeat from * to * until the end of the row.

Row 3: *Knit 1, yarn over forward (i.e., from yourself), slip 2 purlwise (1 stitch and yarn over of the previous row)* repeat from * to * until the end of the row.

Row 4: *Knit 1 together with 2 yarn overs of the previous row, purl 1* repeat from * to * until the end of the row.

Row 5: *Yarn over forward (i.e., from yourself), slip 1 purlwise, knit 1* repeat from * to * until the end of the row.

Row 6: *Purl 1, yarn over forward (i.e., from yourself), slip 2 purlwise (1 stitch and yarn over of the previous row)* repeat from * to * until the end of the row.

Row 7: *Purl 1 together with 2 yarn overs of the previous row, knit 1* repeat from * to * until the end of the row.

Repeat rows: 2-7.

Bind off as follows: slip the edge stitch onto the right needle, knit 1, insert the left needle through the slipped edge stitch from left to right and pass it over the knitted stitch; *now there is 1 stitch on the right needle, knit the next 1, insert the left needle through the 1st stitch from left to right and pass it over the 2nd stitch* repeat from * to * until the end of the row.

Pattern 5

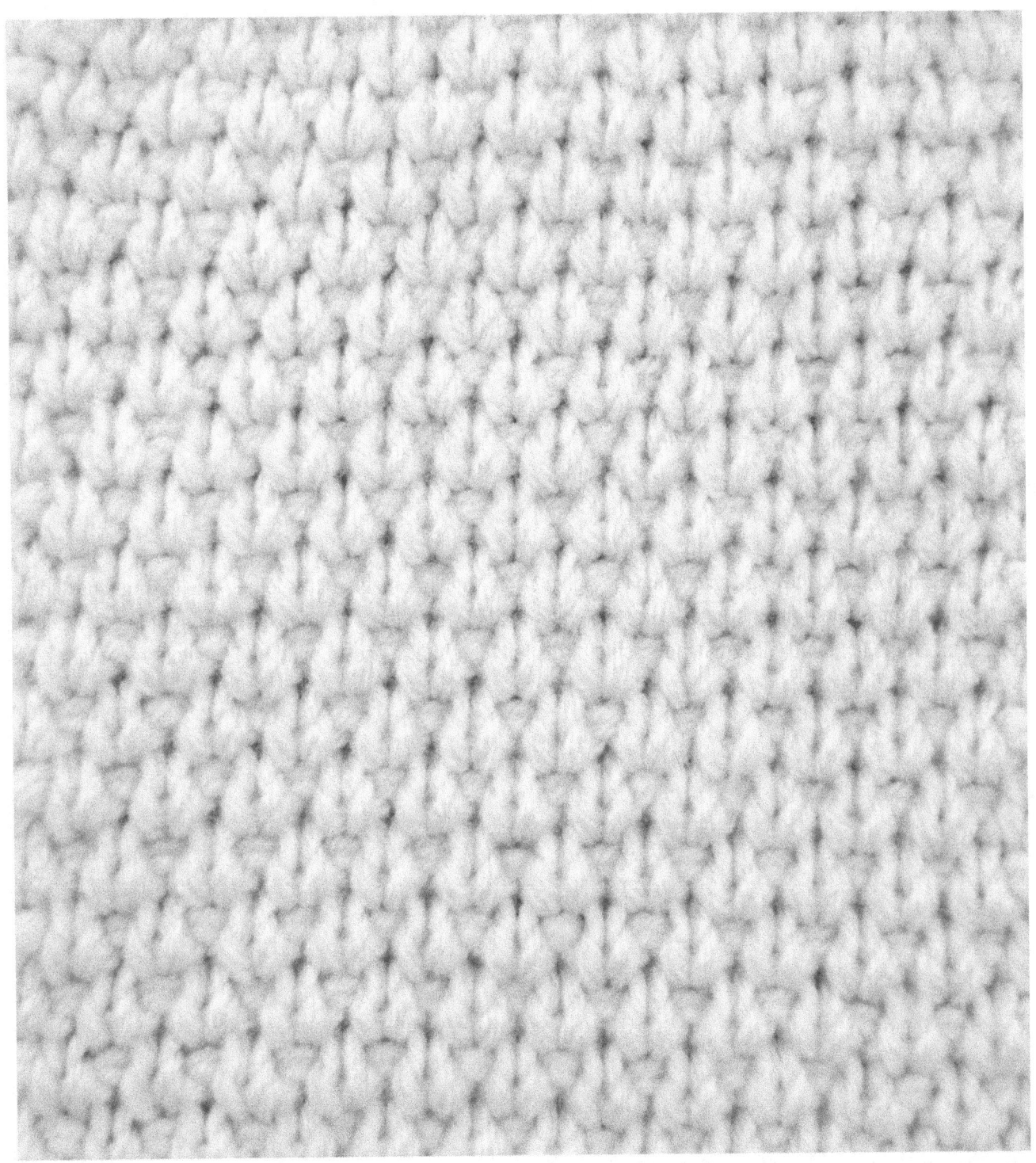

Cast on a multiple of 2, plus 2 edge stitches. Two-stitch repeat. Repeat rows: 1-4. The edge stitches are not included in the description below and must be added. Slip the first edge stitch; purl the last edge stitch as if to

purl in knitting through the back leg as follows: insert the right needle through the stitch from back to front, move the working yarn under the right needle, and pull it with the needle through the stitch. **Needles: U.S. no. 6 (4 mm). Use a bulky yarn.**

Knit through the front leg; purl as follows: with the working yarn in front of the stitch, wrap the working yarn forward (i.e., from yourself) around the tip of the right needle, then pull the yarn with the needle through the stitch. The purl stitch that is worked this way sets up the knit stitch to be knitted through the front leg.

Description:

Row 1: *Yarn over forward (i.e., from yourself), slip 1 purlwise, knit 1* repeat from * to * until the end of the row.

Row 2: *Purl 1, knit 2 together* repeat from * to * until the end of the row.

Row 3: *Knit 1, yarn over forward (i.e., from yourself), slip 1 purlwise* repeat from * to * until the end of the row.

Row 4: *Knit 2 together, purl 1* repeat from * to * until the end of the row.

Repeat rows: 1-4.

Bind off as follows: slip the edge stitch onto the right needle, knit 1, then insert the left needle through the slipped edge stitch from left to right and pass it over the knitted stitch; *now there is 1 stitch on the right needle, knit the next 1, insert the left needle through the 1st stitch from left to right and pass it over the 2nd stitch* repeat from * to * until the end of the row.

Pattern 6

Cast on a multiple of 2, plus 2 edge stitches. Two-stitch repeat. Repeat rows: 1-8. The edge stitches are not included in the description below and must be added. Slip the first edge stitch; purl the last edge stitch as if to

purl in knitting through the back leg as follows: insert the right needle through the stitch from back to front, move the working yarn under the right needle, and pull it with the needle through the stitch.

Knit through the front leg; purl as follows: with the working yarn in front of the stitch, wrap the working yarn forward (i.e., from yourself) around the tip of the right needle, then pull the yarn with the needle through the stitch. The purl stitch that is worked this way sets up the knit stitch to be knitted through the front leg.

Description:

Row 1: *Yarn over forward (i.e., from yourself), slip 1 purlwise, purl 1* repeat from * to * until the end of the row.

Row 2: *Knit 1, yarn over forward (i.e., from yourself), slip 1 with yarn over of the previous row purlwise* repeat from * to * until the end of the row.

Row 3: *With the working yarn in front of your work, slip 1 with 2 yarn overs of the previous rows, purl 1* repeat from * to * until the end of the row.

Row 4: *Knit 1, knit the next triple stitch as 1 stitch (1 stitch with 2 yarn overs of the previous rows)* repeat from * to * until the end of the row.

Row 5: *Purl 1, yarn over forward (i.e., from yourself), slip 1 purlwise* repeat from * to * until the end of the row.

Row 6: *Yarn over yarn over forward (i.e., from yourself), slip 1 stitch with yarn over of the previous row purlwise, knit 1* repeat from * to * until the end of the row.

Row 7: *Purl 1, slip 1 with 2 yarn overs of the previous rows purlwise* repeat from * to * until the end of the row.

Row 8: *Knit triple stitch as 1 stitch (1 stitch with 2 yarn overs of the previous rows), knit 1* repeat from * to * until the end of the row.

Repeat rows: 1-8.

Bind off as follows: slip the edge stitch onto the right needle, knit 1, then insert the left needle through the slipped edge stitch from left to right and pass it over the knitted stitch; *now there is 1 stitch on the right needle, knit the next 1, insert the left needle through the 1st stitch from left to right and pass it over the 2nd stitch* repeat from * to * until the end of the row.

Pattern 7

Cast on a multiple of 2, plus 2 edge stitches. Two-stitch repeat. Repeat rows: 1-4. The edge stitches are not included in the description below and must be added. Slip the first edge stitch; purl the last edge stitch as if to

purl in knitting through the back leg as follows: insert the right needle through the stitch from back to front, move the working yarn under the right needle, and pull it with the needle through the stitch. **Use a bulky yarn. Knit through the front legs.**

Description:

Row 1: Knit all the stitches.

Row 2: *Knit 1, knit the next 1 through the stitch that lies below the stitch on the left needle* repeat from * to * until the end of the row.

Row 3: Knit all the stitches.

Row 4: *Knit 1 through the stitch that lies below the stitch on the left needle, then knit 1* repeat from * to * until the end of the row.

Repeat rows: 1-4.

Bind off as follows: slip the edge stitch onto the right needle, knit 1, then insert the left needle through the slipped edge stitch from left to right and pass it over the knitted stitch; *now there is 1 stitch on the right needle, knit the next 1, insert the left needle through the 1st stitch from left to right and pass it over the 2nd stitch* repeat from * to * until the end of the row.

Pattern 8

Cast on a multiple of 2, plus 2 edge stitches. Two-stitch repeat. Repeat rows: 2-5. The edge stitches are not included in the description below and must be added. Slip the first edge stitch; purl the last edge stitch as if to

purl in knitting through the back leg as follows: insert the right needle through the stitch from back to front, move the working yarn under the right needle, and pull it with the needle through the stitch. **Use a bulky yarn.**

Knit through the front leg, purl as follows: with the working yarn in front of the stitch, wrap the working yarn forward (i.e., from yourself) around the tip of the right needle, then pull the yarn with the needle through the stitch. The purl stitch that is worked this way sets up the knit stitch to be knitted through the front leg.

Description:

Row 1 (set up row): *Slip 1 purlwise, yarn over forward (i.e., from yourself), knit 1* repeat from * to * until the end of the row.

Row 2: *Yarn over forward (i.e., from yourself), slip 1 purlwise, knit 2 together* repeat from * to * until the end of the row.

Row 3: Repeat row 2.

Row 4: *Yarn over forward (i.e., from yourself), slip 1 purlwise, purl 2 together* repeat from * to * until the end of the row.

Row 5: Repeat row 4.

Repeat rows: 2-5.

Bind off as follows: slip the edge stitch onto the right needle, knit 1, then insert the left needle through the slipped edge stitch from left to right and pass it over the knitted stitch; *now there is 1 stitch on the right needle, knit the next 1, insert the left needle through the 1st stitch from left to right and pass it over the 2nd stitch* repeat from * to * until the end of the row.

Pattern 9

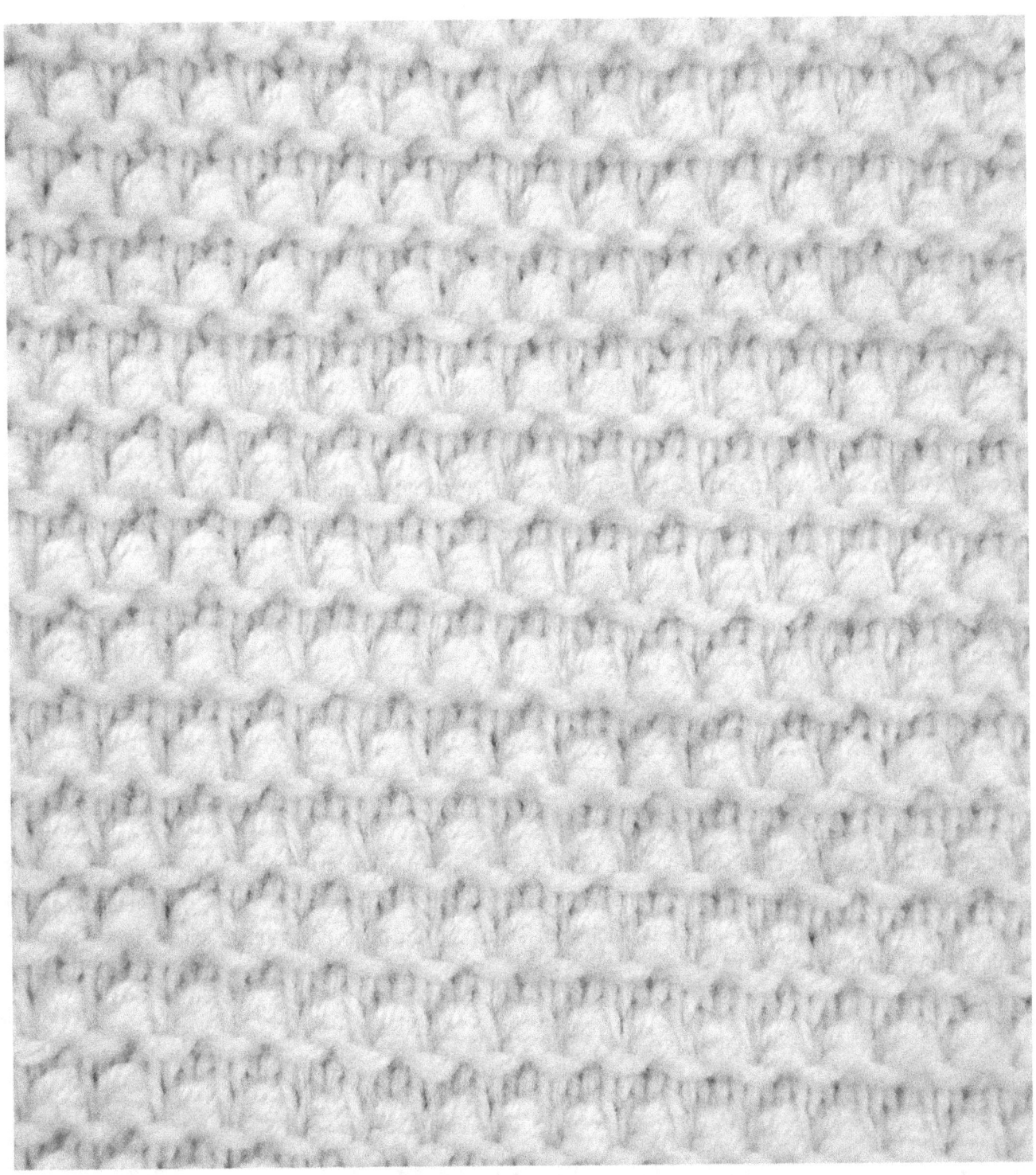

Cast on a multiple of 2, plus 1 for symmetry and 2 edge stitches. Two-stitch repeat. Repeat rows: 3-6. The edge stitches are not included in the description below and must be added. Slip the first edge stitch; purl the last edge stitch.

Knit through the back leg, purl as follows: with the working yarn in front of the stitch, insert the right needle through the stitch from back to front, insert the right needle through the stitch from back to front, move the working yarn under the right needle, and pull it with the needle through the stitch. The purl stitch that is worked this way sets up the knit stitch to be knitted through the back leg.

Description:

Row 1 (set up row): Knit all the stitches.

Row 2 (set up row): Purl all the stitches.

Row 3: *With the working yarn behind your work, slip 1 purlwise, knit 3—loosely—out of the next 1 stitch as follows: knit 1 through the back leg—**do not release the left needle yet**—yarn over forward (i.e., from yourself), knit 1 one more time through the back leg, then release the left needle; now there are 3 stitches knitted out of 1 stitch on the right needle* repeat from * to * until the end of the row before the edge stitch, with the working yarn behind your work, slip 1 purlwise.

Row 4: *With the working yarn behind your work, slip 1 purlwise, knit the next 3 together through the back legs* repeat from * to * until the end of the row before the edge stitch, with the working yarn behind your work, slip 1 purlwise.

Row 5: *Knit 1 through the back leg, knit 1 through the front leg* repeat from * to * until the end of the row before the edge stitch, knit 1 through the back leg.

Row 6: Purl all the stitches.

Repeat rows: 3-6.

Bind off as follows: slip the edge stitch onto the right needle, knit 1, then insert the left needle through the slipped edge stitch from left to right and pass it over the knitted stitch; *now there is 1 stitch on the right needle, knit the next 1, insert the left needle through the 1st stitch from left to right and pass it over the 2nd stitch* repeat from * to * until the end of the row.

Pattern 10

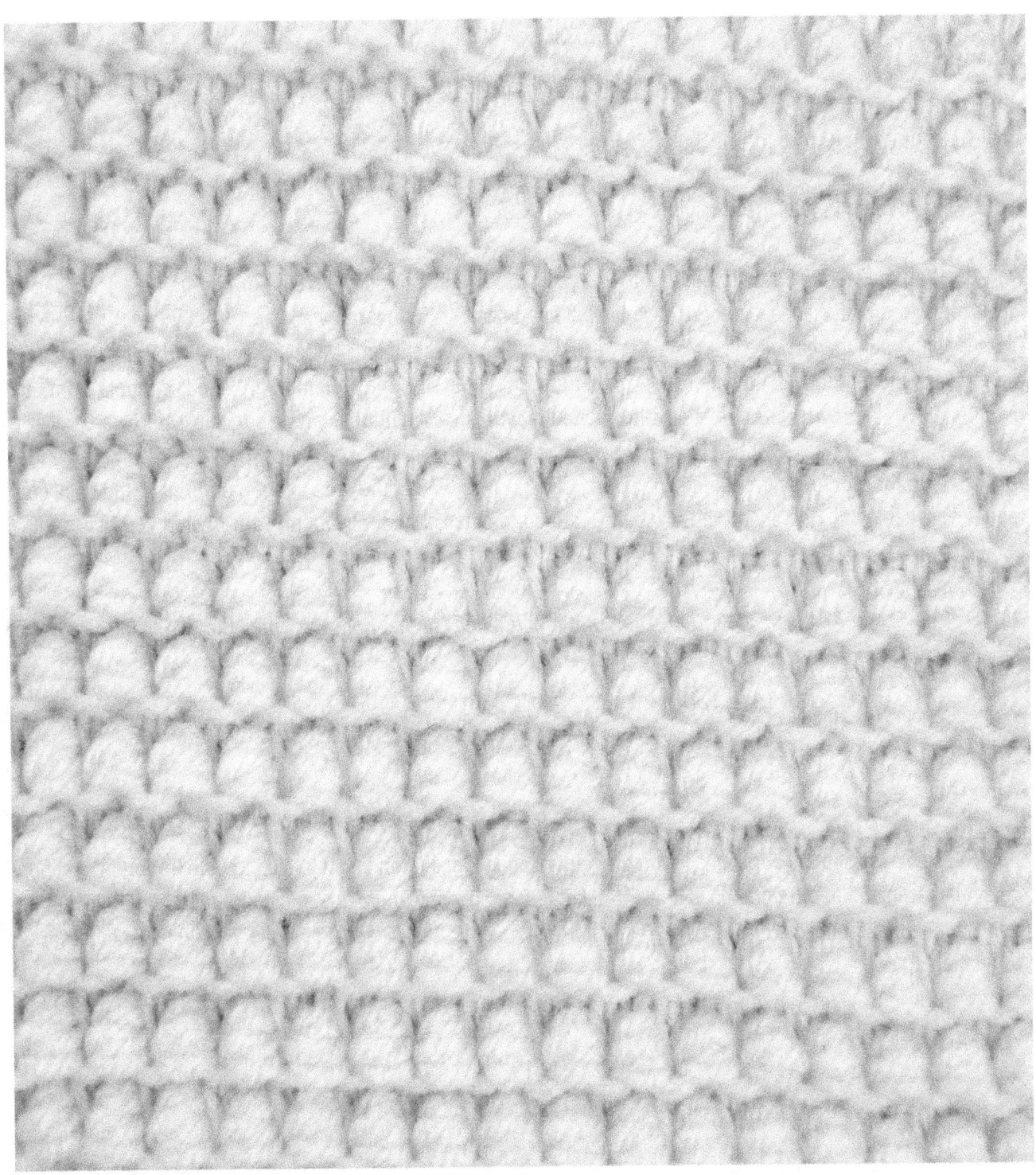

Cast on a multiple of 2, plus 1 for symmetry and 2 edge stitches. Two-stitch repeat. Repeat rows: 3-6. The edge stitches are not included in the description below and must be added. Slip the first edge stitch; purl the last edge stitch.

Knit through the back leg; purl as follows: with the working yarn in front of the stitch, insert the right needle through the stitch from back to front, insert the right needle through the stitch from back to front, move the working yarn under the right needle and pull it with the needle through the stitch. The purl stitch that is worked this way sets up the knit stitch to be knitted through the back leg.

Description:

Row 1 (set up row): Knit all the stitches.

Row 2 (set up row): Purl all the stitches.

Row 3: *With the working yarn behind your work, slip 1 purlwise, knit 5—loosely—out of the next 1 as follows: knit 1 through the back leg—**do not release the left needle yet**—yarn over forward (i.e., from yourself), knit 1 one more time through the back leg, yarn over forward (i.e., from yourself), knit 1 one more time through the back leg, then release the left needle; now there are 5 stitches knitted out of 1 stitch on the right needle* repeat from * to * until the end of the row before the edge stitch, with the working yarn behind your work, slip 1 purlwise.

Row 4: *With the working yarn behind your work, slip 1 purlwise, knit the next 5 together through the back legs* repeat from * to * until the end of the row before the edge stitch, with the working yarn behind your work, slip 1 purlwise.

Row 5: *Knit 1 through the back leg, knit 1 through the front leg* repeat from * to * until the end of the row before the edge stitch, knit 1 through the back leg.

Row 6: Purl all the stitches.

Repeat rows: 3-6.

Bind off as follows: slip the edge stitch onto the right needle, knit 1, then insert the left needle through the slipped edge stitch from left to right and pass it over the knitted stitch; *now there is 1 stitch on the right needle, knit the next 1, insert the left needle through the 1st stitch from left to right and pass it over the 2nd stitch* repeat from * to * until the end of the row.

Pattern 11

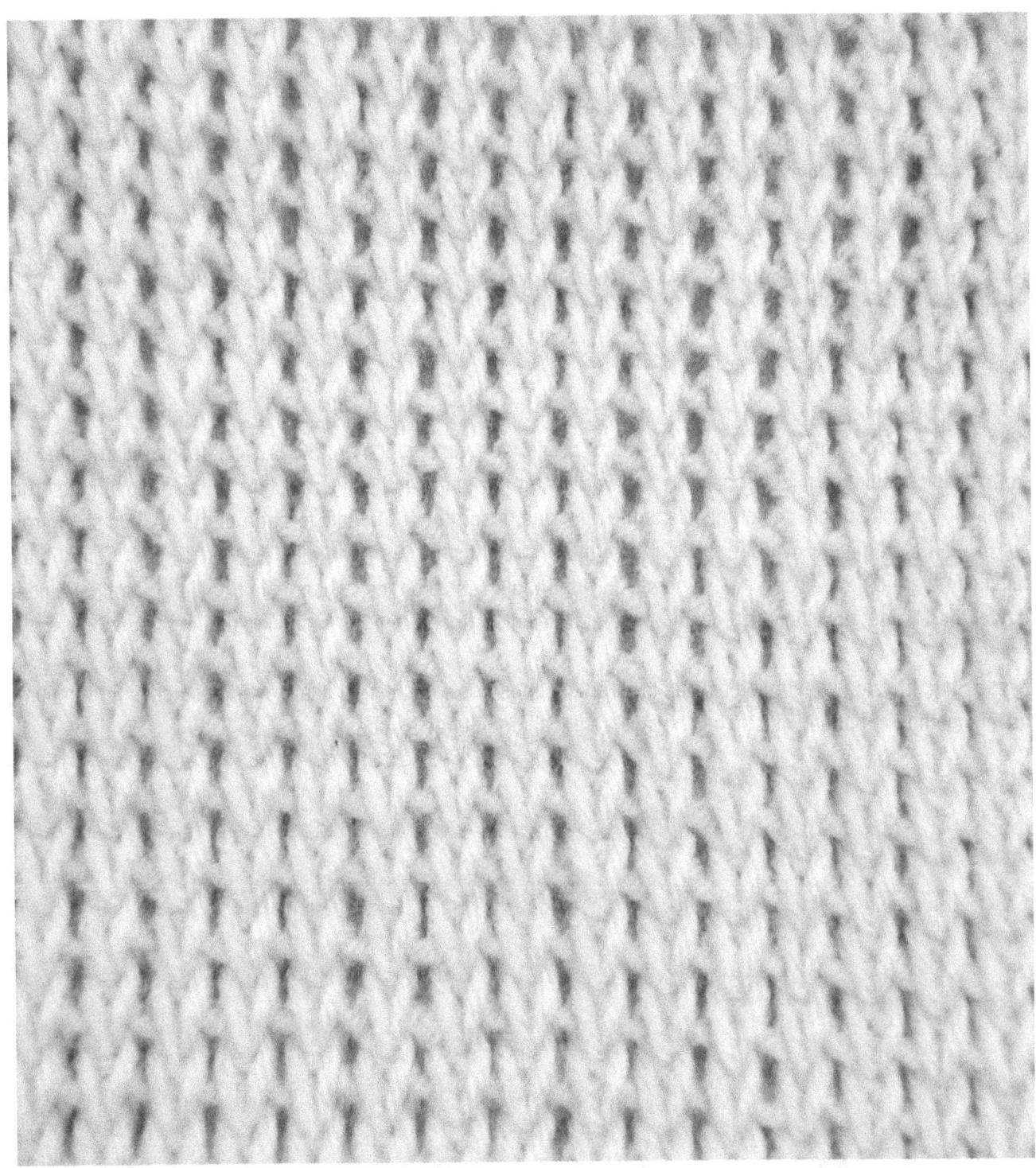

Cast on a multiple of 3, plus 2 edge stitches. Three-stitch repeat. Repeat rows: 1-2. The edge stitches are not included in the description below and must be added. Slip the first edge stitch; purl the last edge stitch as if to

purl in knitting through the back leg as follows: insert the right needle through the stitch from back to front, move the working yarn under the right needle, and pull it with the needle through the stitch.

Note: Knit all stitches the same length.

Description:

Row 1: *Knit 3 together through the back legs as follows: knit 3 together through the back legs—**do not release the left needle yet**—yarn over forward (i.e., from yourself), knit 3 together through the back legs 1 more time then release the left needle* repeat from * to * until the end of the row.

Row 2: *Knit 2 through the front legs, with the working yarn in front of your work slip 1 purlwise* repeat from * to * until the end of the row.

Repeat rows: 1-2.

Bind off as follows: after the last row on the Front Side, turn your work over; the Back Side: slip all the stitches from the left needle to the right one; thus, the working yarn is at the end of the row; turn your work over; the Front Side: slip 2 stitches from the left needle to the right one, insert the left needle through the 1st slipped stitch from left to right, and pass it over the 2nd one (now there is 1 stitch on the right needle), *slip 1 stitch from the left needle to the right one, insert the left needle through the 1st stitch on the right needle from left to right and pass it over the 2nd one; now there is 1 stitch on the right needle* repeat from * to * until the end of the row.

Note: Bind off using larger needles than the working ones to create a larger chain of edge stitches for trimming, as this method of binding off stitches creates a tight chain of edge stitches.

Pattern 12

Option 1

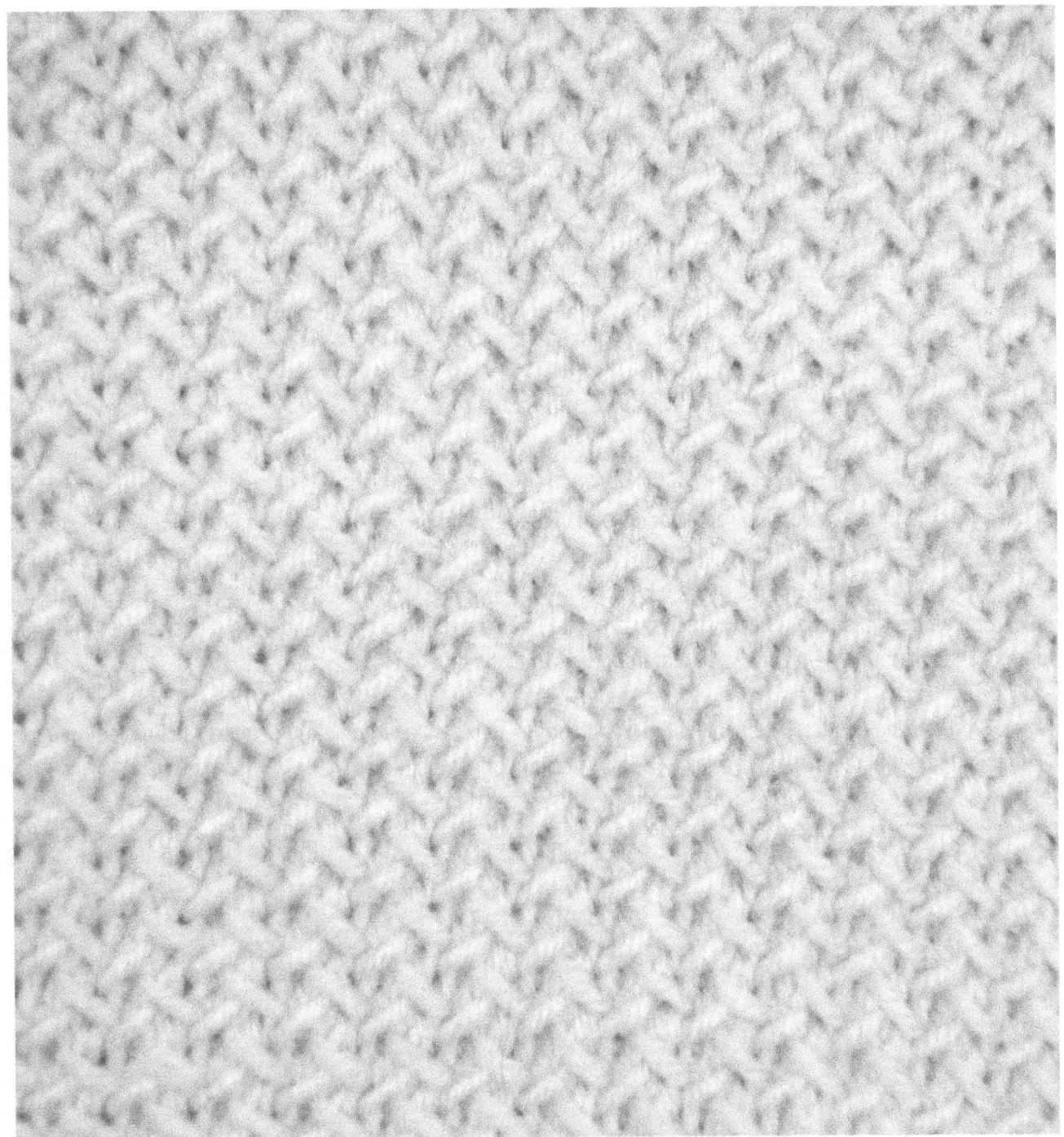

Cast on a multiple of 3, plus 1 for symmetry and 2 edge stitches. Three-stitch repeat. Repeat rows: 1-2. The edge stitches are not included in the description below and must be added. Slip the first edge stitch; purl the last edge stitch as if to purl in knitting through the back leg as follows: insert the right needle through the stitch from back to front, move the working yarn under the right needle, and pull it with the needle through the stitch.

Knit through the front leg; purl as follows: with the working yarn in front of the stitch, wrap the working yarn forward (i.e., from yourself) around the tip of the right needle, then pull the yarn with the needle through the stitch. The purl stitch that is worked this way sets up the knit stitch to be knitted through the front leg.

Description:

Row 1: Knit 1 through the front leg, *yarn over forward (i.e., from yourself), slip 1 purlwise, knit 2 through the front legs, then insert the left needle through the slipped stitch and pass it over the 2 knitted stitches* repeat from * to * until the end of the row.

Row 2: Purl 1, *yarn over forward (i.e., from yourself), move the working yarn forward, then with the yarn in front of the next stitch, slip 1 purlwise, purl 2, then insert the left needle through the slipped stitch and pass it over the 2 knitted stitches* repeat from * to * until the end of the row.

Repeat rows: 1-2.

Bind off as follows: after the last row 1, turn your work over; the Back Side: slip all the stitches from the left needle to the right one; thus, the working yarn is at the end of the row; turn your work over; the Front Side: slip 2 stitches from the left needle to the right one, insert the left needle through the 1st slipped stitch from left to right and pass it over the 2nd one (now there is 1 stitch on the right needle), *slip 1 stitch from the left needle to the right one, insert the left needle through the 1st stitch on the right needle from left to right and pass it over the 2nd one; now there is 1 stitch on the right needle* repeat from * to * until the end of the row.

Note: Bind off using larger needles than the working ones to create a larger chain of edge stitches for trimming, as this method of binding off stitches creates a tight chain of edge stitches.

Option 2

Knit the same as described in option 1 using a bulky yarn.

Pattern 13

Option 1

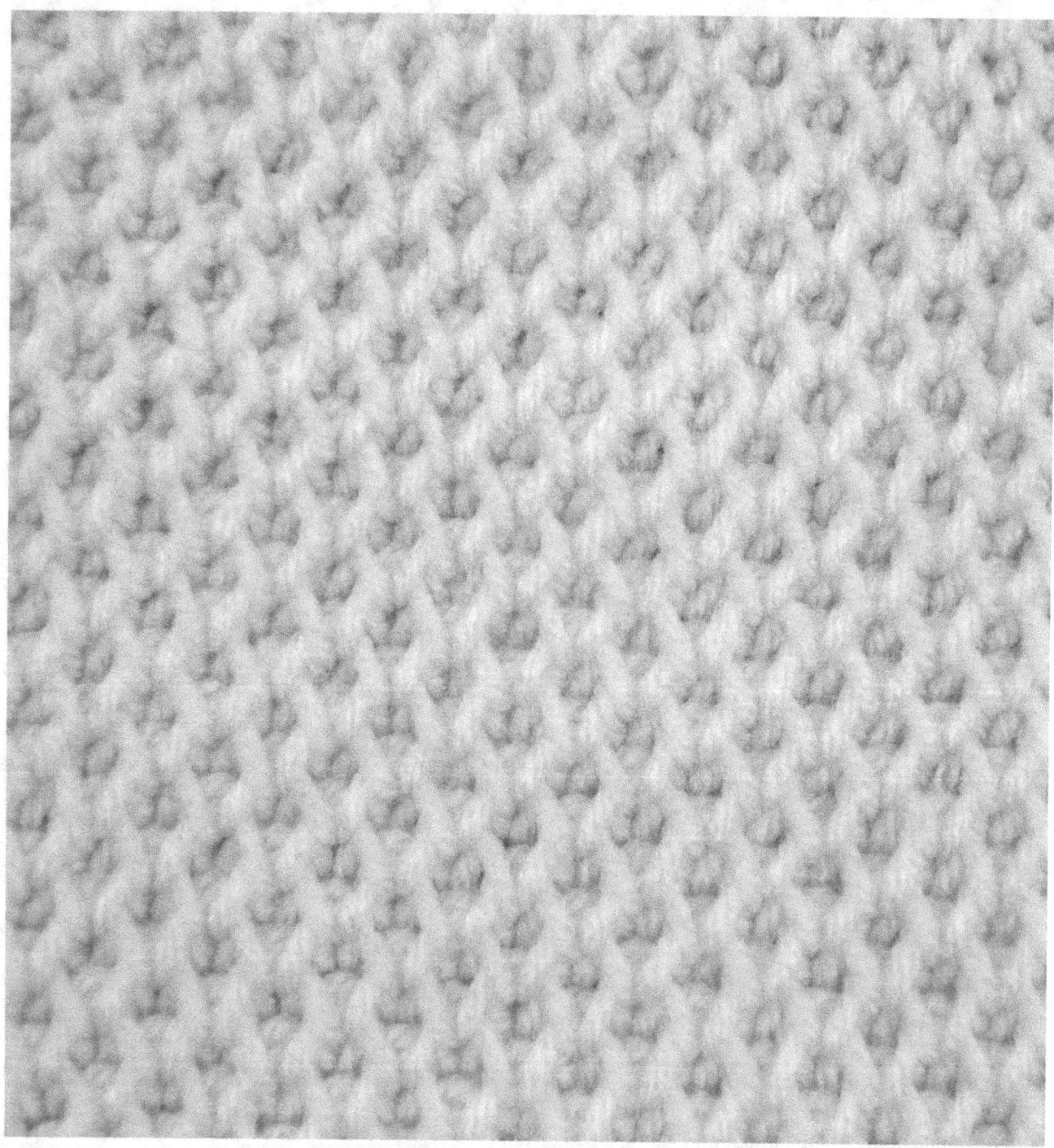

Cast on a multiple of 2, plus 2 edge stitches. Two-stitch repeat. Repeat rows: 2-5. The edge stitches are not included in the description below and must be added. Slip the first edge stitch; purl the last edge stitch as if to

purl in knitting through the back leg as follows: insert the right needle through the stitch from back to front, move the working yarn under the right needle, and pull it with the needle through the stitch.

Knit through the front leg; purl as follows: with the working yarn in front of the stitch, wrap the working yarn forward (i.e., from yourself) around the tip of the right needle, then pull the yarn with the needle through the stitch. The purl stitch that is worked this way sets up the knit stitch to be knitted through the front leg. **Needles: U.S. no. 10 (5.75 mm).**

Description:

Row 1 (set up row): Knit all the stitches.

Row 2: *Knit 1, knit 1 through the previous row's stitch, inserting the right needle through the stitch below the stitch on the left needle* repeat from * to * until the end of the row.

Row 3: *Knit 1, knit 1 through the previous row's stitch as described in row 2* repeat from * to * until the end of the row.

Row 4: *Knit 1 through the previous row's stitch as described in row 2, knit 1* repeat from * to * until the end of the row.

Row 5: *Knit 1 through the previous row's stitch as described in row 2, knit 1* repeat from * to * until the end of the row.

Repeat rows: 2-5.

Bind off after the last row 5 as follows: slip the edge stitch onto the right needle, purl 1, then insert the left needle through the slipped edge stitch from left to right and pass it over the purled stitch; *now there is 1 stitch on the right needle, purl the next 1, insert the left needle through the 1st stitch from left to right and pass it over the 2nd stitch* repeat from * to * until the end of the row.

Option 2

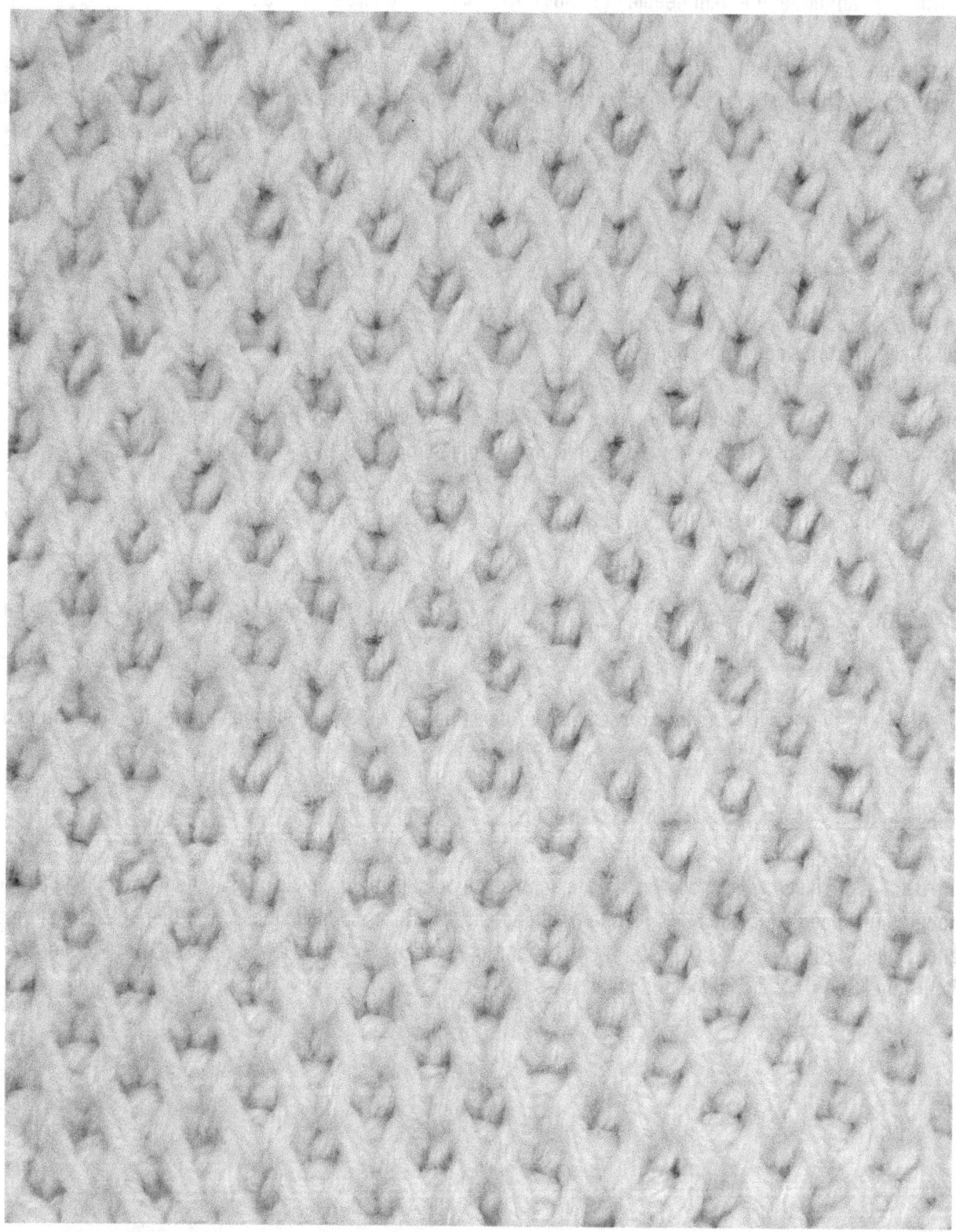

Knit the same as described in option 1 using a bulky yarn.

Pattern 14

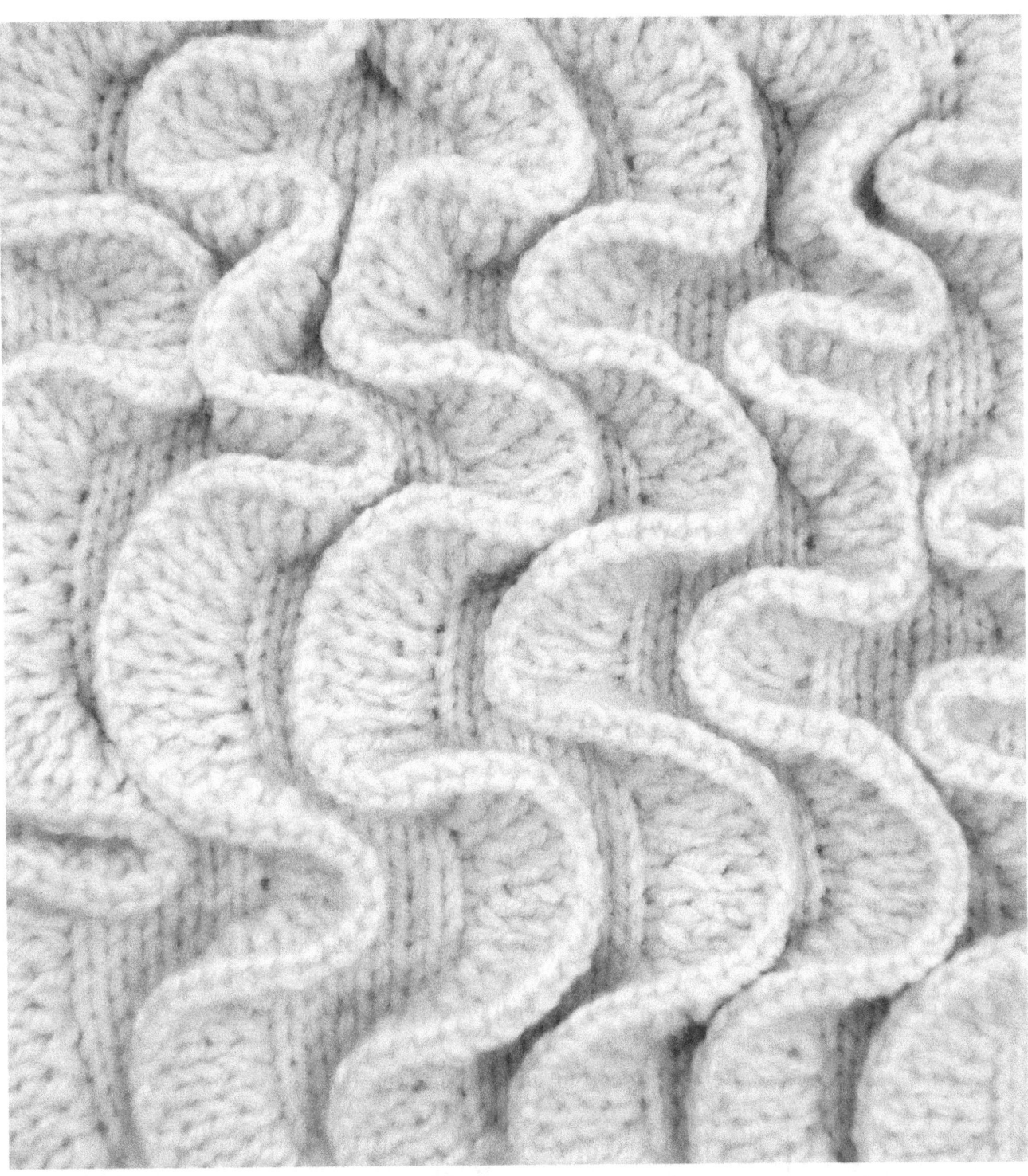

Cast on a multiple of 6, plus 2 edge stitches. The edge stitches are not included in the description below and must be added. Slip the first edge stitch; purl the last edge stitch.

Knit through the back leg; purl as follows: with the working yarn in front of the stitch, insert the right needle through the stitch from back to front, move the working yarn under the right needle, and pull it with the needle through the stitch. The purl stitch that is worked this way sets up the knit stitch to be knitted through the back leg.

Note: Knit folds on circular needles. Knit folds without the edge stitches. Repeat folds in every 6th vertical row.

Description:

Knit a base for the future folds as follows:

Row 1: Knit all the stitches.

Row 2: Purl all the stitches.

Repeat rows: 1-2 until the required length.

Bind off as follows: slip the edge stitch onto the right needle, knit 1, then insert the left needle through the slipped edge stitch from left to right and pass it over the knitted stitch; *now there is 1 stitch on the right needle, knit the next 1, insert the left needle through the 1st stitch on the right needle from left to right and pass it over the 2nd stitch* repeat from * to * until the end of the row.

Folds:

1. Pick up—vertically—onto circular needles 1 leg of each stitch in every 6th row in the direction from bottom to top.

2. Increase the number of stitches as follows:

Row 1: Make 3 stitches out of 1 stitch: knit 1—**do not release the left needle yet**— yarn over forward (i.e., from yourself), knit 1, then release the left needle, purl 1* repeat from * to * until the end of the row.

Row 2: *Knit 1, purl 1, knit 1, purl 1* repeat from * to * until the end of the row.

Row 3: *Knit 1, purl 1, knit 1, purl 1* repeat from * to * until the end of the row.

Row 4: *Knit 1, purl 1, knit 1, purl 1* repeat from * to * until the end of the row.

Row 5: *Knit 1, purl 1, knit 1, purl 1* repeat from * to * until the end of the row.

Row 6: Do not turn your work over. Move all the stitches onto the opposite end of the circular needles. Now the working yarn is at the end of the row.

Bind off all the stitches as follows: slip 2 purlwise from the left needle to the right one, insert the left needle from left to right through the 1st slipped stitch, and pass it over the 2nd stitch (now there is 1 stitch on the right needle); *slip 1 from the left needle to the right one, insert the left needle from left to right through the 1st stitch and pass it over the 2nd stitch, now there is one stitch on the right needle* repeat from * to * until the end of the row.

Repeat the fold in every 6th row.

Pattern 15

Cast on a multiple of 5, plus 2 edge stitches. The edge stitches are not included in the description below and must be added. Slip the first edge stitch; purl the last edge stitch. **Knit through the back leg, purl as follows:** with the working yarn in front of the stitch, insert the right needle through the stitch from back to front, move the working yarn under the right needle, and pull it with the needle through the stitch. The purl stitch that is worked this way sets up the knit stitch to be knitted through the back leg.

Note: Knit folds without the edge stitches. Knit folds on circular needles. Repeat folds every 5 vertical rows.

Description:

1. Knit a base for folds:

Row 1: Knit all the stitches.

Row 2: Purl all the stitches.

Repeat rows: 1-2 until the required length.

Bind off as follows: slip the edge stitch onto the right needle, knit 1, then insert the left needle through the slipped edge stitch from left to right and pass it over the knitted stitch; *now there is 1 stitch on the right needle, knit the next 1, insert the left needle through the 1st stitch from left to right and pass it over the 2nd stitch* repeat from * to * until the end of the row.

2. Folds:

Row 1: Pick up onto circular needles 1 leg of each stitch in every 5th vertical row in the direction from bottom to top. Increase the number of stitches, making 3 out of each 1 stitch as follows: *knit 1—do not release the left needle yet—yarn over forward (i.e., from yourself), knit 1, then release the left needle, purl 1* repeat from * to * until the end of the row.

Row 2: *Knit 1, purl 1, knit 1, purl 1* repeat from * to * until the end of the row.

Row 3: *Knit 1, purl 1, knit 1, purl 1* repeat from * to * until the end of the row.

Row 4: *Knit 1, purl 1, knit 1, purl 1* Repeat from * to * until the end of the row.

Row 5: *Knit 1, purl 1, knit 1, purl 1* Repeat from * to * until the end of the row.

Row 6: Do not turn your work over. Move all the stitches to the opposite end of the circular needles; thus, the working yarn is at the end of the row.

Bind off as follows: slip 2 purlwise from the left needle to the right one, insert the left needle through the 1st stitch from left to right, and pass it over the 2nd stitch (now there is 1 stitch on the right needle); *slip 1 purlwise from the left needle to the right one, insert the left needle through the 1st stitch from left to right and pass it over the 2nd stitch* repeat from * to * until the end of the row.

Repeat rows: 1-6 every 5 vertical rows.

Pattern 16

Cast on a multiple of 2, plus 2 edge stitches. Two-stitch repeat. Repeat rows: 1-24. The edge stitches are not included in the description below and must be added. Slip the first edge stitch; purl the last edge stitch.

Knit through the back leg, purl as follows: with the working yarn in front of the stitch, insert the right needle through the stitch from back to front, move the working yarn under the right needle, and pull it with the needle through the stitch. The purl stitch that is worked this way sets up the knit stitch to be knitted through the back leg.

Description:

Row 1: *Knit 1, with the working yarn behind your work slip 1 purlwise* repeat from * to * until the end of the row.

Row 2: *Purl 1 through the back leg, slip 1 purlwise* repeat from * to * until the end of the row.

Row 3: *Knit 1, make 1 additional stitch* repeat from * to * until the end of the row. **Knit tightly.**

Row 4: Purl all the stitches.

Row 5: Knit all the stitches.

Row 6: Purl all the stitches.

Row 7-22: Alternate rows 5-6.

Row 23: *Knit 2 together as follows: insert the right needle through the 1st stitch from back to front and slip it onto the right needle, insert the right needle through the 2nd stitch from back to front and slip it onto the right needle, return both stitches onto the left needle, then knit 2 together through the front legs* repeat from * to * until the end of the row. **Knit tightly.**

Row 24: Purl all the stitches.

Repeat rows: 1-24.

Bind off after the last row 2 as follows: slip the edge stitch onto the right needle, knit 1, then insert the left needle through the slipped edge stitch from left to right and pass it over the knitted stitch; *now there is 1 stitch on the right needle, knit the next 1, insert the left needle through the 1st stitch from left to right and pass it over the 2nd stitch* repeat from * to * until the end of the row.

Pattern 17

Cast on a multiple of 10, plus 2 edge stitches. Ten-stitch repeat. Repeat rows: 1-4. The edge stitches are not included in the description below and must be added. Slip the first edge stitch; purl the last edge stitch.

Knit through the back leg; purl as follows: with the working yarn in front of the stitch, insert the right needle through the stitch from back to front, move the working yarn under the right needle, and pull it with the needle through the stitch. The purl stitch that is worked this way sets up the knit stitch to be knitted through the back leg. **Needles:** U.S. no. 7 (4.5 mm).

Description:

Row 1: *Knit 1 as follows: insert the right needle through the back leg from front to back and wrap the working yarn forward (i.e., from yourself) around the tip of the right needle 3 times, then pull the needle through the stitch, as usual, these 3 stitches count as 1 stitch* repeat from * to * until the end of the row.

Row 2: *With the working yarn behind your work, slip 10 purlwise from the left needle to the right one, simultaneously unrolling these stitches. Then, return these 10 elongated stitches onto the left needle. Insert the right needle through the 6th, 7th, 8th, 9th, and 10th stitches and pass them over the 5th, 4th, 3rd, 2nd, and 1st. Now there are 5 stitches on the left needle and 5 stitches on the right needle, which are intersecting each other. Return the other 5 stitches onto the left needle. Now purl each of these 10 stitches* repeat from * to * until the end of the row.

Row 3: Repeat row 1.

Row 4: Purl the first 5, simultaneously unrolling these stitches. *With the working yarn behind your work, slip 10 purlwise from the left needle to the right one, simultaneously unrolling these stitches. Insert the left needle through the first 5 elongated stitches, counting from the right side, and pass them over the other 5. Now there are 5 stitches on the left needle and 5 stitches on the right needle, which are intersecting each other. Slip the 5 stitches that are on the right needle onto the left needle. Purl, each of these 10 stitches* repeat from * to * until the end of the row before the edge stitch, purl the last 5, simultaneously unrolling these stitches.

Repeat rows: 1-4.

Bind off as follows: after the last row 4, turn your work over; the Front Side: slip all the stitches from the left needle to the right one; thus, the working yarn is at the end of the row; turn your work over; the Back Side: slip 2 stitches from the left needle to the right one, insert the left needle through the 1st slipped stitch from left to right and pass it over the 2nd one; now there is 1 stitch on the right needle; *slip 1 stitch from the left needle to the right one, insert the left needle through the 1st stitch on the right needle from left to right and pass it over the 2nd one; now there is 1 stitch on the right needle* repeat from * to * until the end of the row.

Note: Bind off using larger needles than the working ones to create a larger chain of edge stitches for trimming, as this method of binding off stitches creates a tight chain of edge stitches.

Pattern 18

Reversible

Cast on a multiple of 2, plus 2 edge stitches. Two-stitch repeat. Repeat row 1. The edge stitches are not included in the description below and must be added. Slip the first edge stitch; purl the last edge stitch as if to purl in knitting through the back leg as follows: insert the right needle through the stitch from back to front, move the working yarn under the right needle, and pull it with the needle through the stitch.

Description:

Row 1: *With the working yarn behind the stitch, slip 1 purlwise, knit the next 1 through the front leg, then insert the left needle through the slipped stitch from left to right, pass it over the knitted stitch—and still keeping the slipped stitch on the left needle—knit it through the front leg* repeat from * to * until the end of the row.

Repeat row 1.

Bind off as follows: after the last row, turn your work over; slip all the stitches from the left needle to the right one; thus, the working yarn is at the end of the row; turn your work over; slip 2 stitches from the left needle to the right one; insert the left needle through the 1st slipped stitch from left to right and pass it over the 2nd one (now there is 1 stitch on the right needle); *slip 1 stitch from the left needle to the right one; insert the left needle through the 1st stitch on the right needle from left to right and pass it over the 2nd one; now there is 1 stitch on the right needle* repeat from * to * until the end of the row.

Note: Bind off using larger needles than the working ones to create a larger chain of edge stitches for trimming, as this method of binding off stitches creates a tight chain of edge stitches.

Pattern 19

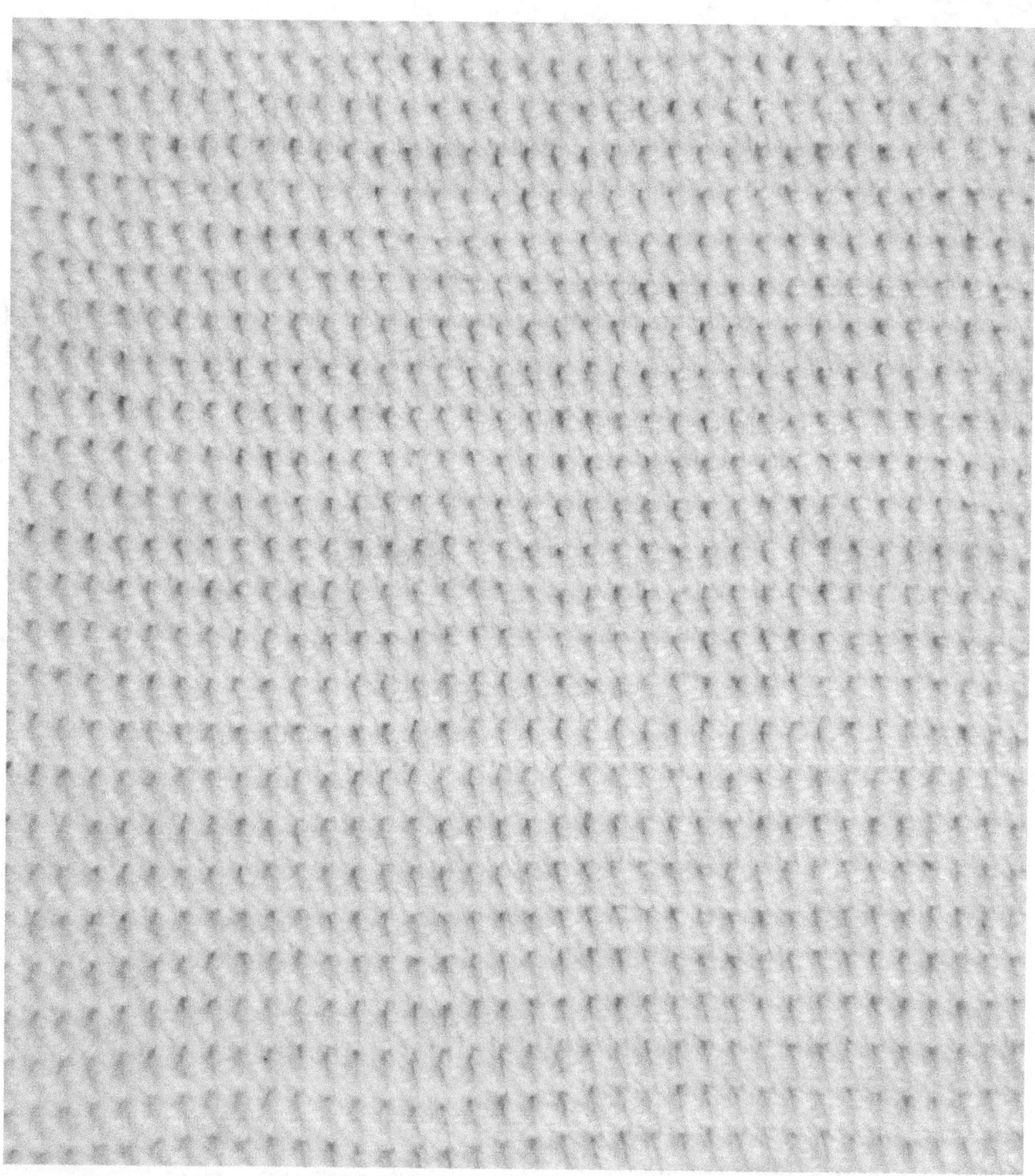

Cast on any number of stitches, plus 2 edge stitches. Repeat rows: 1-2. The edge stitches are not included in the description below and must be added. **Knit the first edge stitch through the back leg; knit the last edge stitch through the back leg.**

Description:

Row 1 (Back Side): *Yarn over forward (i.e., from yourself), with the working yarn behind your work, slip 1 stitch purlwise* repeat from * to * until the end of the row.

Row 2 (Front Side): *Knit 2 together through the back legs* repeat from * to * until the end of the row.

Repeat rows: 1-2.

Bind off as follows: after the last row 2, turn your work over; the Back Side: slip all the stitches from the left needle to the right one; thus, the working yarn is at the end of the row; turn your work over; the Front Side: slip 2 stitches from the left needle to the right one, insert the left needle through the 1st slipped stitch from left to right and pass it over the 2nd one (now there is 1 stitch on the right needle); *slip 1 stitch from the left needle to the right one, insert the left needle through the 1st stitch on the right needle from left to right and pass it over the 2nd one; now there is 1 stitch on the right needle* repeat from * to * until the end of the row.

Note: Bind off using larger needles than the working ones to create a larger chain of edge stitches for trimming, as this method of binding off stitches creates a tight chain of edge stitches.

Pattern 20

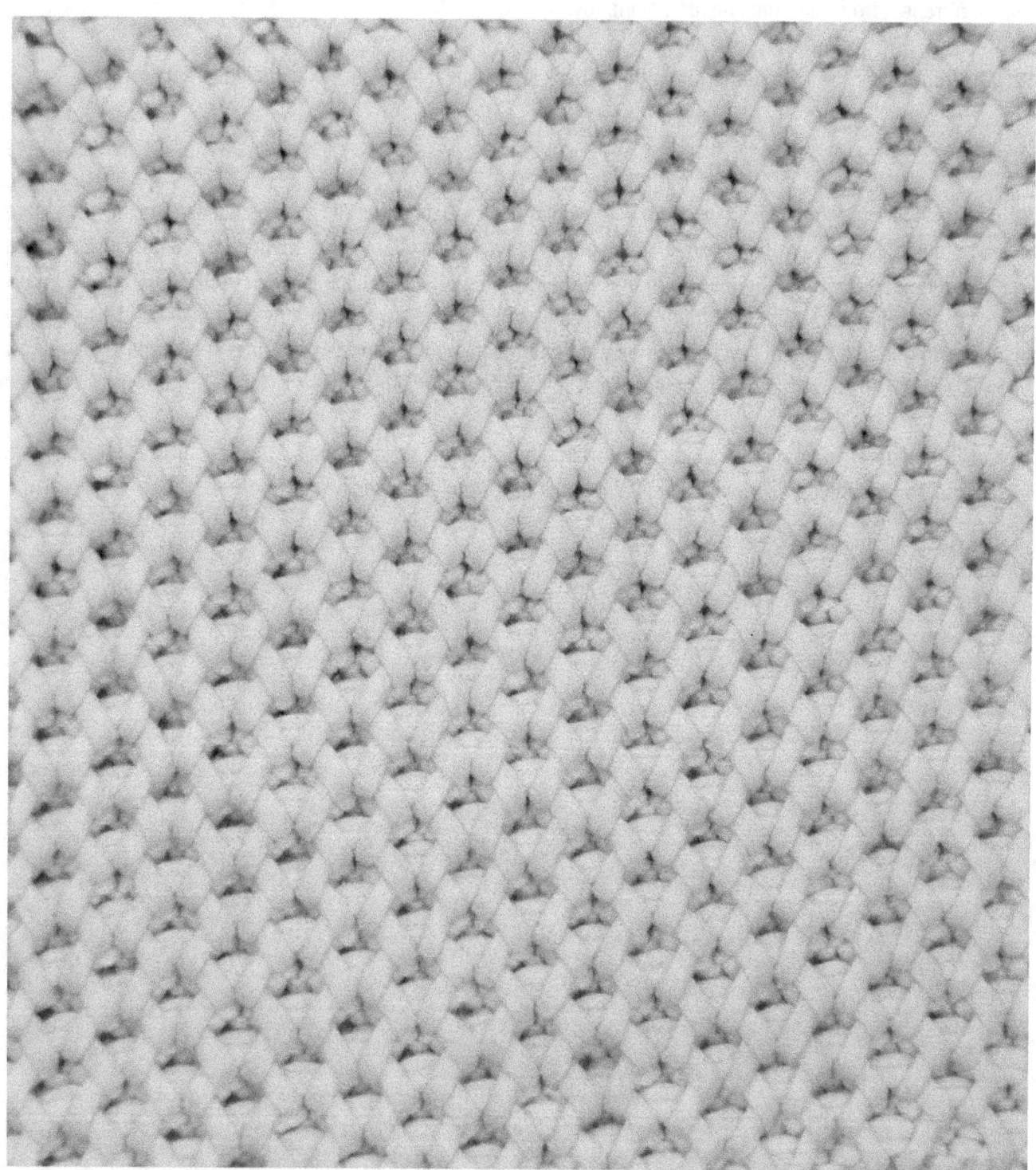

Cast on a multiple of 4, plus 2 for symmetry and 2 edge stitches. Two-stitch repeat. Repeat row: 3-6. The edge stitches are not included in the description below and must be added. Slip the first edge stitch; **purl the last edge**

stitch as if to purl in knitting through the back leg as follows: insert the right needle through the stitch from back to front, move the working yarn under the right needle, and pull it with the needle through the stitch.

Knit through the front leg; purl as follows: with the working yarn in front of the stitch, wrap the working yarn forward (i.e., from yourself) around the tip of the right needle, then pull the working yarn with the needle through the stitch. The purl stitch that is worked this way sets up the knit stitch to be knitted through the front leg. **Use a bulky yarn.**

Description:

Row 1: *Knit 2, with the working yarn in front of your work slip 2* repeat from * to * until the end of the row before the edge stitch, knit 2.

Row 2: *Purl 2, with the working yarn behind your work slip 2* repeat from * to * until the end of the row before the edge stitch, purl 2.

Row 3: *With the working yarn in front of your work slip 2, knit the next 1 together with 2 slipped stitches in the 2 previous rows as follows: pick up 2 slipped stitches in 2 rows below onto the right needle, inserting the right needle in the direction going up, then insert the right needle through the front leg of the stitch that is on the left needle and knit 1 together with these 2 slipped stitches (i.e., knit 3 together), knit the next 1 together with the same 2 slipped stitches, the same as the 1st stitch* repeat from * to * until the end of the row before the edge stitch, with the working yarn in front of the stitch, slip the last 2.

Row 4: *With the working yarn behind your work, slip 2, purl 2* repeat from * to * until the end of the row before the edge stitch, with the working yarn behind your work slip 2.

Row 5: *Knit 1 together with 2 slipped stitches in 2 previous rows as described in row 3, knit the next 1 together with the same 2 slipped stitches in 2 previous rows as described in row 3, then with the working yarn in front of your work, slip 2* repeat from * to * until the end of the row before the edge stitch, knit 1 together with 2 slipped stitches in 2 previous rows, then knit the next 1 together with the same 2 slipped stitches in 2 previous rows.

Row 6: *Purl 2, with the working yarn behind your work slip 2* repeat from * to * until the end of the row before the edge stitch, purl 2.

Repeat rows: 3-6.

Bind off through the back legs as follows: Slip the edge stitch onto the right needle, knit 1, then insert the left needle through the slipped edge stitch from left to right and pass it over the knitted stitch; *now there is 1 stitch on the right needle, knit the next 1, insert the left needle through the 1st stitch from left to right and pass it over the 2nd stitch* repeat from * to * until the end of the row.

Pattern 21

Cast on a multiple of 2, plus 2 edge stitches. Two-stitch repeat. Repeat rows: 1-2. The edge stitches are not included in the description and must be added. Slip the first edge stitch; purl the last edge stitch.

Knit through the back leg; purl as follows: insert the right needle through the stitch from back to front, move the working yarn under the right needle, and pull it with the needle through the stitch. The purl stitch that is worked this way sets up the knit stitch to be knitted through the back leg. **Needles: U.S. no. 7 (4.5 mm).**

Description:

Row 1: *Knit 2 as follows: *insert the right needle through the back leg of the 2nd stitch and roll the working yarn forward (i.e., from yourself) onto the right needle 2 times, then finish knitting this stitch as usual (thus, the received stitch is rolled on the right needle twice), then knit the 1st stitch the same as the 2nd stitch* repeat from * to * until the end of the row.

Row 2: Purl 1 as follows: with the working yarn in front of the stitch, slip 1 onto the right needle, simultaneously unrolling this elongated stitch, then return this elongated stitch onto the left needle, insert the right needle purlwise through this stitch and roll the working yarn **backward (i.e., to yourself)** on the needle 2 times, then pull it with the needle through the stitch (thus, the received stitch is rolled on the right needle twice) *purl 2 as follows: slip 2 onto the right needle, simultaneously unrolling these 2 stitches, return both stitches onto the left needle, insert the right needle through the 2nd stitch purlwise and roll the working yarn **backward (i.e., to yourself)** on the right needle 2 times, then pull it with the needle through the stitch (thus, the received stitch is rolled on the right needle twice)—**do not release the left needle yet**—purl the 1st stitch the same as the 2nd stitch, then release the left needle* repeat from * to * until the end of the row before the edge stitch, purl 1 the same as the 1st stitch as described above.

Repeat rows: 1-2.

Bind off as follows: after the last row 2, turn your work over; the Front Side: slip all the stitches from the left needle to the right one, simultaneously unrolling elongated stitches; now the working yarn is at the end of the row; turn your work over; the Back Side: slip 2 stitches from the left needle to the right one, insert the left needle through the 1st slipped stitch from left to right and pass it over the 2nd one; now there is 1 stitch on the right needle; *slip 1 stitch from the left needle to the right one, insert the left needle through the 1st stitch on the right needle from left to right and pass it over the 2nd one; now there is 1 stitch on the right needle* repeat from * to * until the end of the row.

Note: Bind off using larger needles than the working ones to create a larger chain of edge stitches for trimming, as this method of binding off stitches creates a tight chain of edge stitches.

Pattern 22

Reversible

Cast on a multiple of 2, plus 2 edge stitches. Two-stitch repeat. Repeat rows: 1-2. The edge stitches are not included in the description below and must be added. **Knit the first edge stitch through the back leg; knit the last**

edge stitch through the back leg.

Purl all the stitches as follows: with the working yarn in front of the stitch, insert the right needle through the stitch from back to front, move the working yarn under the right needle, and pull it with the needle through the stitch. The purl stitch that is worked this way sets up the knit stitch to be knitted through the back leg. **Use a bulky yarn.**

Description:

Row 1: *Knit 1 through the front leg, purl 1 through the back leg* repeat from * to * until the end of the row.

Row 2: *Purl 1 through the back leg, knit 1 through the front leg* repeat from * to * until the end of the row.

Repeat rows: 1-2.

Bind off after the last row 2 as follows: slip the edge stitch onto the right needle, knit 1, then insert the left needle through the slipped edge stitch from left to right and pass it over the knitted stitch; *now there is 1 stitch on the right needle, knit the next 1, insert the left needle through the 1st stitch from left to right and pass it over the 2nd stitch* repeat from * to * until the end of the row.

Pattern 23

Cast on a multiple of 3, plus 2 edge stitches. Three-stitch repeat. Repeat rows: 1-4. The edge stitches are not included in the description below and must be added. Slip the first edge stitch, purl the last edge stitch as if to

purl in knitting through the back leg as follows: insert the right needle through the stitch from back to front, move the working yarn under the right needle, and pull it with the needle through the stitch.

Knit through the front leg; purl as follows: with the working yarn in front of the stitch, wrap the working yarn forward (i.e., from yourself) around the tip of the right needle, then pull the working yarn with the needle through the stitch. The purl stitch that is worked this way sets up the knit stitch to be knitted through the front leg.

Note: Do not tighten the working yarn behind slipped stitches. Knit the slipped stitches loosely. Use a bulky yarn.

Description:

Row 1: *With the working yarn behind your work, slip 1 purlwise, knit 2* repeat from * to * until the end of the row.

Row 2: Knit all the stitches.

Row 3: *Knit 2, with the working yarn behind your work slip 1 purlwise* repeat from * to * until the end of the row.

Row 4: Knit all the stitches.

Repeat rows: 1-4.

Bind off as follows: slip the edge stitch onto the right needle, knit 1, then insert the left needle through the slipped edge stitch from left to right and pass it over the knitted stitch; *now there is 1 stitch on the right needle, knit the next 1, insert the left needle through the 1st stitch from left to right and pass it over the 2nd stitch* repeat from * to * until the end of the row.

Pattern 24

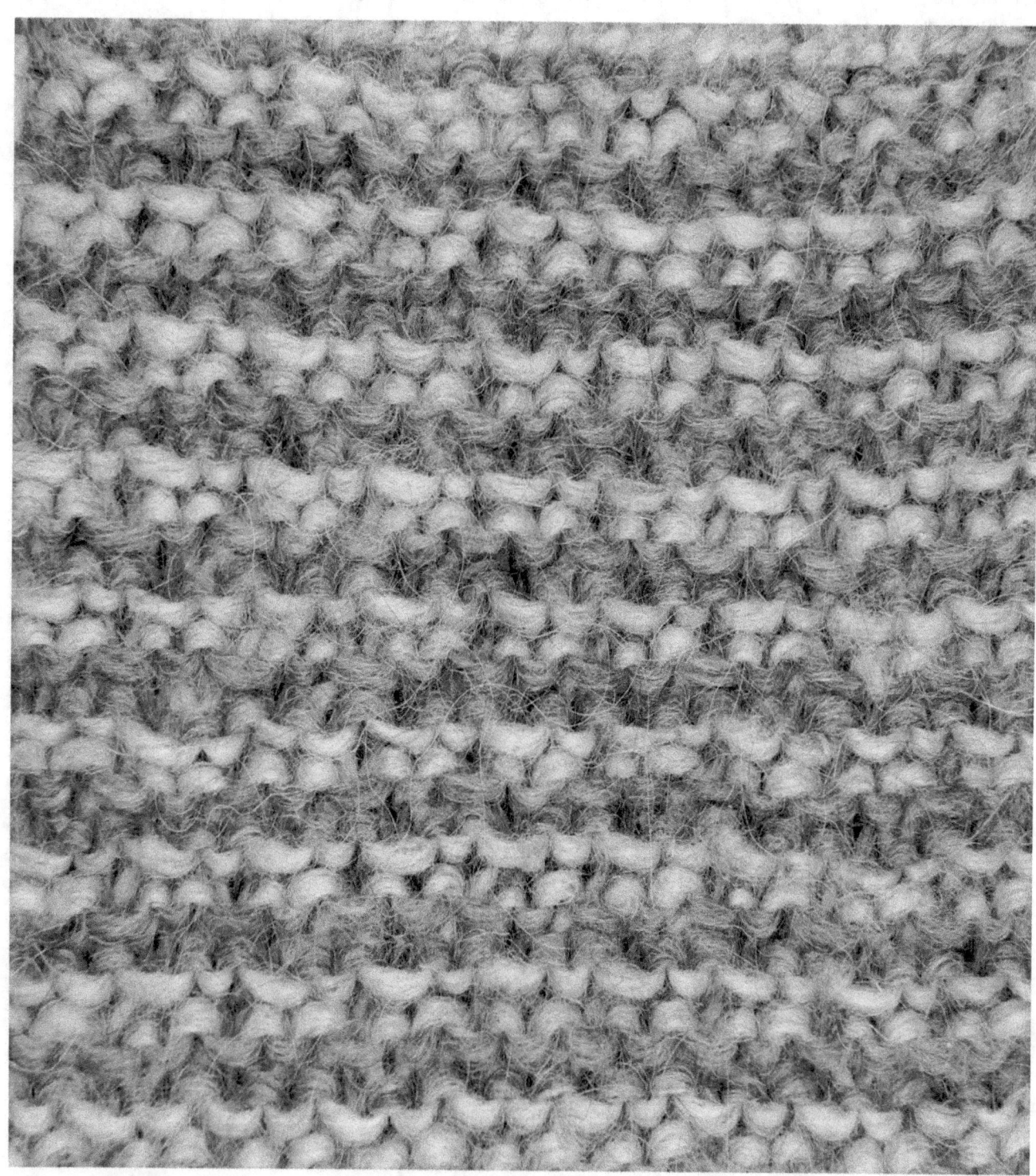

Cast on a multiple of 3, plus 2 edge stitches. Three-stitch repeat. Repeat rows: 1-4. The edge stitches are not included in the description below and must be added. Slip the first edge stitch; purl the last edge stitch as if to

purl in knitting through the back leg as follows: insert the right needle through the stitch from back to front, move the working yarn under the right needle, and pull it with the needle through the stitch.

Knit through the front leg; purl as follows: with the working yarn in front of the stitch, wrap the working yarn forward (i.e., from yourself) around the tip of the right needle, then pull the working yarn with the needle through the stitch. The purl stitch that is worked this way sets up the knit stitch to be knitted through the front leg.

Note: Do not tighten the working yarn behind slipped stitches. Knit the slipped stitches loosely. Use a bulky yarn.

Description:

Row 1 (Color A): *With the working yarn behind your work, slip 1 purlwise, knit 2* repeat from * to * until the end of the row.

Row 2 (Color A): Knit all the stitches.

Row 3 (Color B): Knit the edge stitch, *knit 2, with the working yarn behind your work slip 1 purlwise* repeat from * to * until the end of the row.

Row 4 (Color B): Knit all the stitches.

Repeat rows: 1-4.

Bind off as follows: slip the edge stitch onto the right needle, knit 1, then insert the left needle through the slipped edge stitch from left to right and pass it over the knitted stitch; *now there is 1 stitch on the right needle, knit the next 1, insert the left needle through the 1st stitch from left to right and pass it over the 2nd stitch* repeat from * to * until the end of the row.

Pattern 25

Cast on a multiple of 4, plus 1 and 2 edge stitches. Four-stitch repeat. Repeat rows: 1-2. The edge stitches are not included in the description below and must be added. Slip the first edge stitch; purl the last edge stitch as if

to purl in knitting through the back leg as follows: insert the right needle through the stitch from back to front, move the working yarn under the right needle, and pull it with the needle through the stitch.

Knit through the front leg; purl as follows: with the working yarn in front of the stitch, wrap the working yarn forward (i.e., from yourself) around the tip of the right needle, then pull the working yarn with the needle through the stitch. The purl stitch that is worked this way sets up the knit stitch to be knitted through the front leg.

Note: Do not tighten the working yarn behind slipped stitches. Knit the slipped stitches loosely. Use a bulky yarn.

Description:

Row 1: *Knit 1, with the working yarn behind your work slip 3 purlwise* repeat from * to * until the end of the row before the edge stitch, knit 1.

Row 2: Knit all the stitches.

Repeat rows: 1-2.

Bind off as follows: slip the edge stitch onto the right needle, knit 1, insert the left needle through the slipped edge stitch from left to right and pass it over the knitted stitch; *now there is 1 stitch on the right needle, knit the next 1, insert the left needle through the 1st stitch from left to right and pass it over the 2nd stitch* repeat from * to * until the end of the row* repeat from * to * until the end of the row.

Pattern 26

Cast on a multiple of 5, plus 2 edge stitches. Five-stitch repeat. Repeat rows: 1-4. The edge stitches are not included in the description below and must be added. Slip the first edge stitch; purl the last edge stitch as if to

purl in knitting through the back leg as follows: insert the right needle through the stitch from back to front, move the working yarn under the right needle, and pull it with the needle through the stitch.

Knit through the front leg; purl as follows: with the working yarn in front of the stitch, wrap the working yarn forward (i.e., from yourself) around the tip of the right needle, then pull the working yarn with the needle through the stitch. The purl stitch that is worked this way sets up the knit stitch to be knitted through the front leg.

Note: Do not tighten the working yarn behind slipped stitches. Knit the slipped stitches loosely. Use a bulky yarn.

Description:

Row 1: *Knit 3, with the working yarn behind your work slip 2 purlwise* repeat from * to * until the end of the row.

Row 2: Knit all the stitches.

Row 3: *With the working yarn behind your work, slip 2 purlwise, knit 3* repeat from * to * until the end of the row.

Row 4: Knit all the stitches.

Repeat rows: 1-4.

Bind off as follows: slip the edge stitch onto the right needle, knit 1, insert the left needle through the slipped edge stitch from left to right and pass it over the knitted stitch; *now there is 1 stitch on the right needle, knit the next 1, insert the left needle through the 1st stitch from left to right and pass it over the 2nd stitch* repeat from * to * until the end of the row* repeat from * to * until the end of the row.

Pattern 27

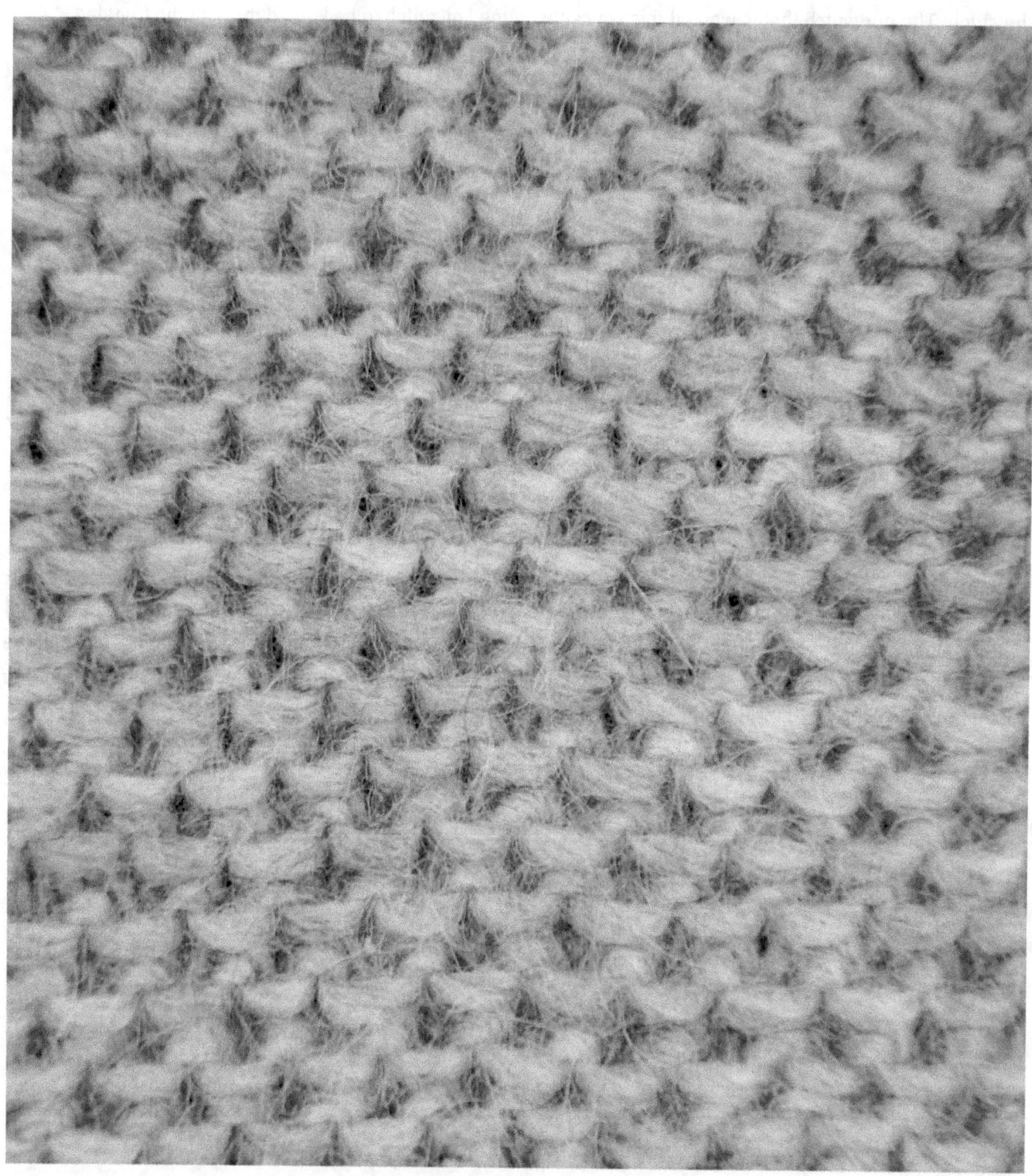

Cast on a multiple of 2, plus 2 edge stitches. Two-stitch repeat. Repeat rows: 1-4. The edge stitches are not included in the description below and must be added. Slip the first edge stitch; purl the last edge stitch as if to

purl in knitting through the back leg as follows: insert the right needle through the stitch from back to front, move the working yarn under the right needle, and pull it with the needle through the stitch.

Knit through the front leg; purl as follows: with the working yarn in front of the stitch, wrap the working yarn forward (i.e., from yourself) around the tip of the right needle, then pull the working yarn with the needle through the stitch. The purl stitch that is worked this way sets up the knit stitch to be knitted through the front leg.

Note: Do not tighten the working yarn behind slipped stitches. Knit the slipped stitches loosely. Use a bulky yarn.

Description:

Row 1: *Knit 1, with the working yarn behind your work, slip 1 purlwise* repeat from * to * until the end of the row.

Row 2: Knit all the stitches.

Row 3: *With the working yarn behind your work, slip 1 purlwise, knit 1* repeat from * to * until the end of the row.

Row 4: Knit all the stitches.

Repeat rows: 1-4.

Bind off as follows: slip the edge stitch onto the right needle, knit 1, then insert the left needle through the slipped edge stitch from left to right and pass it over the knitted stitch; *now there is 1 stitch on the right needle, knit the next 1, insert the left needle through the 1st stitch from left to right and pass it over the 2nd stitch* repeat from * to * until the end of the row.

Pattern 28

Cast on a multiple of 2, plus 1 and 2 edge stitches. Two-stitch repeat. Repeat rows: 1-2. The edge stitches are not included in the description below and must be added. Slip the first edge stitch; purl the last edge stitch.

Knit through the back leg; purl as follows: with the working yarn in front of the stitch, insert the right needle through the stitch from back to front, move the working yarn under the right needle, and pull it with the needle through the stitch. The purl stitch that is worked this way sets up the knit stitch to be knitted through the back leg. **Use a bulky yarn.**

Description:

Row 1 (Back Side): *Purl 2 together as follows: purl 2 together, then purl the first stitch 1 more time* repeat from * to * until the end of the row before the edge stitch, purl 1.

Row 2 (Front Side): *Slip 1 purlwise, knit the next 1, yarn over forward (i.e., from yourself), then pass the slipped stitch over the 2 stitches (1 knitted stitch and yarn over)* repeat from * to * until the end of the row before the edge stitch, knit 1.

Repeat rows: 1-2.

Bind off as follows: after the last row 2, turn your work over; the Back Side: slip all the stitches from the left needle to the right one; thus, the working yarn is at the end of the row; turn your work over; the Front Side: slip 2 stitches from the left needle to the right one, insert the left needle through the 1st slipped stitch from left to right and pass it over the 2nd stitch, (now there is 1 stitch on the right needle); *slip 1 stitch from the left needle to the right one, insert the left needle through the 1st stitch on the right needle from left to right and pass it over the 2nd stitch; now there is 1 stitch on the right needle* repeat from * to * until the end of the row.

Note: Bind off using larger needles than the working ones to create a larger chain of edge stitches for trimming, as this method of binding off stitches creates a tight chain of edge stitches.

Pattern 29

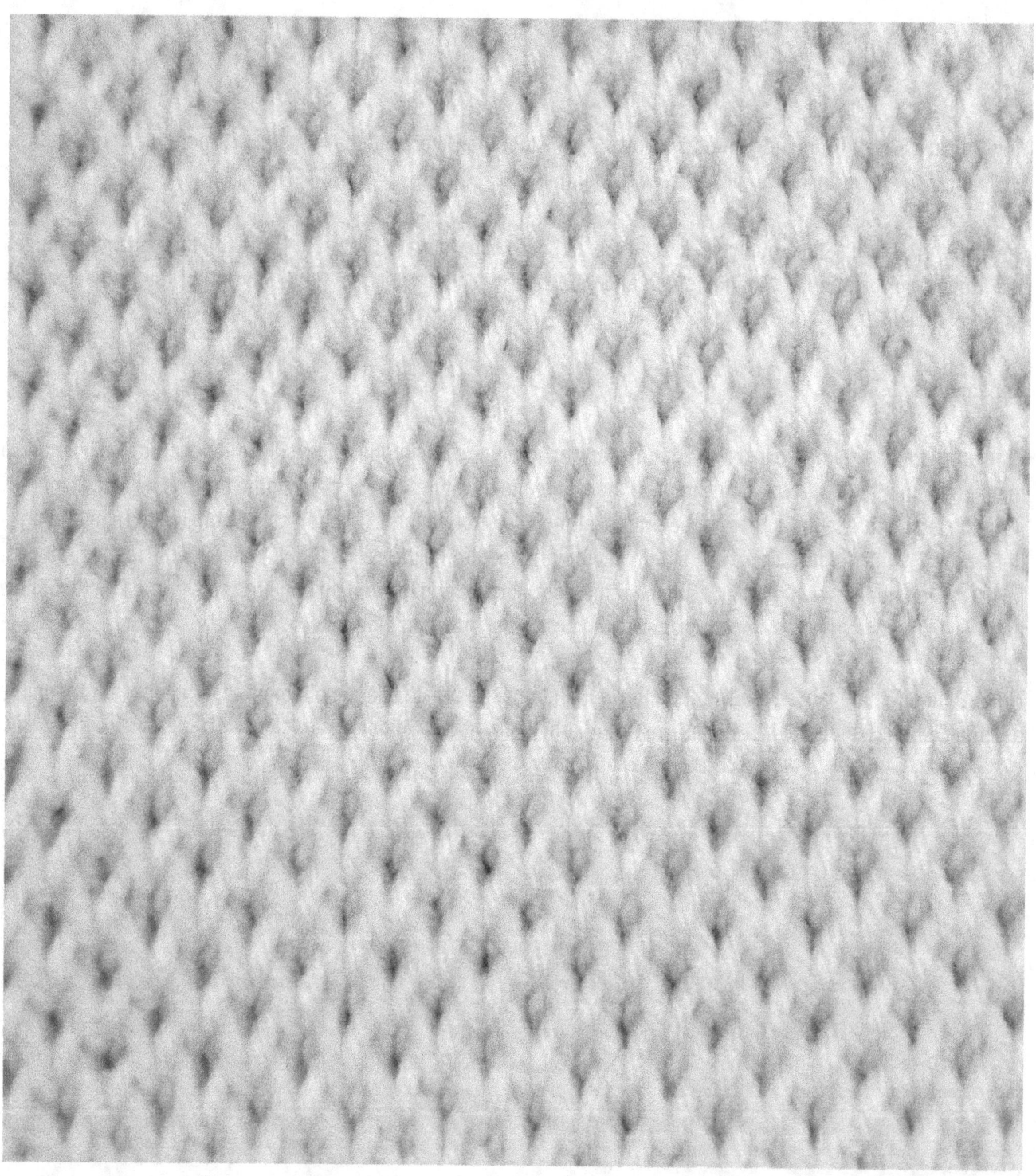

Cast on a multiple of 2, plus 2 edge stitches. Two-stitch repeat. Repeat rows: 2-5. The edge stitches are not included in the description below and must be added. Slip the first edge stitch; purl the last edge stitch as if to

purl in knitting through the back leg as follows: insert the right needle through the stitch from back to front, move the working yarn under the right needle, and pull it with the needle through the stitch.

Knit through the front leg; purl as follows: with the working yarn in front of the stitch, wrap the working yarn forward (i.e., from yourself) around the tip of the right needle, then pull the working yarn with the needle through the stitch. The purl stitch that is worked this way sets up the knit stitch to be knitted through the front leg.

Description:

Row 1 (set up row): *Knit 1, yarn over forward (i.e., from yourself), slip 1 purlwise* repeat from * to * until the end of the row.

Row 2: *Knit 2 together (1 stitch and yarn over of the previous row), yarn over forward (i.e., from yourself), slip 1 purlwise* repeat from * to * until the end of the row.

Row 3: Knit 1, *slip 1 purlwise (yarn over of the previous row), knit 2* repeat from * to * until the end of the row before the edge stitch, slip 1 purlwise (yarn over of the previous row), knit 1.

Row 4: *Yarn over forward (i.e., from yourself), slip 1 purlwise, knit 2 together (yarn over of the previous row and 1 stitch)* repeat from * to * until the end of the row.

Row 5: *Knit 2, slip 1 purlwise (yarn over of the previous row)* repeat from * to * until the end of the row.

Repeat rows: 2-5.

Bind off as follows: after the last row 5, turn your work over; the Back Side: slip all the stitches from the left needle to the right one; thus, the working yarn is at the end of the row; turn your work over; the Front Side: slip 2 stitches from the left needle to the right one, insert the left needle through the 1st slipped stitch from left to right and pass it over the 2nd stitch; now there is 1 stitch on the right needle; *slip 1 stitch from the left needle to the right one, insert the left needle through the 1st stitch on the right needle from left to right and pass it over the 2nd stitch; now there is 1 stitch on the right needle* repeat from * to * until the end of the row.

Note: Bind off using larger needles than the working ones to create a larger chain of edge stitches for trimming, as this method of binding off stitches creates a tight chain of edge stitches.

Pattern 30

Cast on a multiple of 2, plus 1 and 2 edge stitches. Two-stitch repeat. Repeat rows: 1-4. The edge stitches are not included in the description below and must be added. Slip the first edge stitch; purl the last edge stitch as if

to purl in knitting through the back leg as follows: insert the right needle through the stitch from back to front, move the working yarn under the right needle, and pull it with the needle through the stitch.

Knit through the front leg; purl as follows: with the working yarn in front of the stitch, wrap the working yarn forward (i.e., from yourself) around the tip of the right needle, then pull the working yarn with the needle through the stitch. The purl stitch that is worked this way sets up the knit stitch to be knitted through the front leg. **Use a bulky yarn.**

Description:

Row 1: Knit all the stitches.

Row 2: Knit all the stitches.

Row 3: *Knit 1, then with the working yarn in front of your work, slip 1 purlwise* repeat from * to * until the end of the row before the edge stitch, knit 1.

Row 4: *Purl 1, with the working yarn behind your work, slip 1 purlwise* repeat from * to * until the end of the row before the edge stitch, purl 1.

Repeat rows: 1-4.

Bind off after the last 4 as follows: slip the edge stitch onto the right needle, knit 1, then insert the left needle through the slipped edge stitch from left to right and pass it over the knitted stitch; *now there is 1 stitch on the right needle, knit the next 1, then insert the left needle from left to right through the 1st stitch on the right needle and pass it over the 2nd stitch* repeat from * to * until the end of the row.

Pattern 31

Cast on a multiple of 2, plus 1 for symmetry and 2 edge stitches. Two-stitch repeat. Repeat rows: 1-2. Slip the first edge stitch; purl the last edge stitch.

Knit through the back leg; purl as follows: with the working yarn in front of your work, insert the right needle through the stitch from back to front, move the working yarn under the right needle, and pull it with the needle through the stitch. The purl stitch that is worked this way sets up the knit stitch to be knitted through the back leg. **Use a bulky yarn.**

Description:

Row 1: *Purl 1, knit 1* repeat from * to * until the end of the row before the edge stitch, purl 1.

Row 2: *Knit 1, with the working yarn behind your work slip 1 knitwise* repeat from * to * until the end of the row before the edge stitch, knit 1.

Repeat rows: 1-2.

Bind off as follows: slip the edge stitch onto the right needle, knit the next 1 through the front leg, then insert the left needle through the slipped edge stitch from left to right and pass it over the knitted stitch; *now there is 1 stitch on the right needle; knit the next 1 through the front leg, (now there are 2 stitches on the right needle); insert the left needle through the 1st stitch on the right needle from left to right and pass it over the 2nd stitch* repeat from * to * until the end of the row.

Pattern 32

Reversible

Cast on any number of stitches, plus 2 edge stitches. One-stitch repeat. Repeat row 1. Slip the first edge stitch; purl the last edge stitch as if to purl in knitting through the back leg as follows: insert the right needle through the stitch from back to front, move the working yarn under the right needle, and pull it with the needle through the stitch. **Knit through the front legs.**

Description:

Row 1: Knit 1 through the front leg.

Repeat row 1.

Bind off as follows: slip the edge stitch onto the right needle, knit 1, then insert the left needle through the slipped edge stitch from left to right and pass it over the knitted stitch; *now there is 1 stitch on the right needle; knit the next 1, then insert the left needle through the 1st stitch on the right needle from left to right, and pass it over the 2nd stitch* repeat from * to * until the end of the row.

Pattern 33

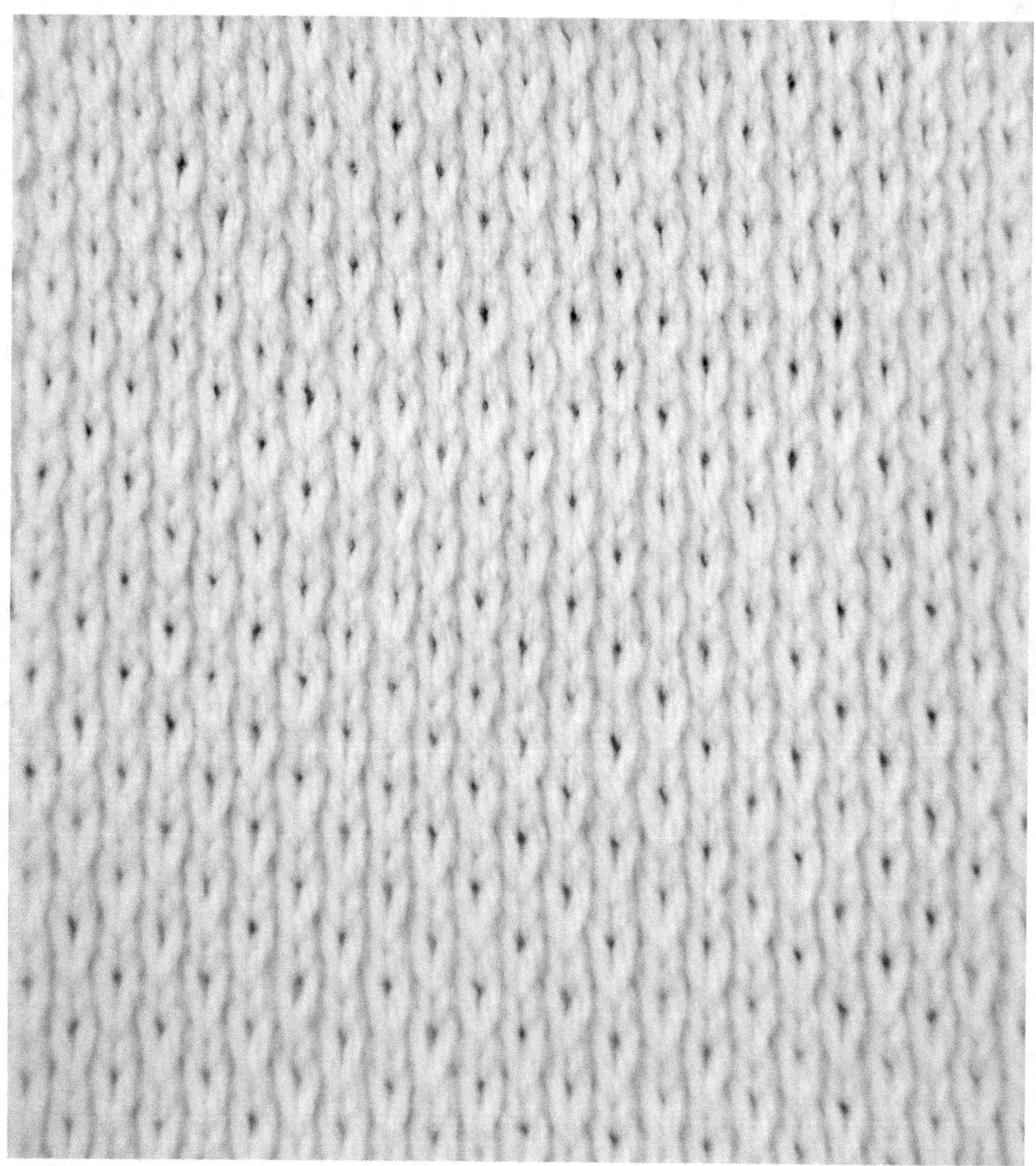

Cast on a multiple of 4, plus 3 and 2 edge stitches. Four-stitch repeat. Repeat rows: 1-4. The edge stitches are not included in the description below and must be added. Slip the first edge stitch; purl the last edge stitch as if

to purl in knitting through the back leg as follows: insert the right needle through the stitch from back to front, move the working yarn under the right needle, and pull it with the needle through the stitch.

Knit through the front leg; purl as follows: with the working yarn in front of the stitch, wrap the working yarn forward (i.e., from yourself) around the tip of the right needle, then pull the working yarn with the needle through the stitch. The purl stitch that is worked this way sets up the knit stitch to be knitted through the front leg.

Description:

Row 1: Knit 1, with the working yarn behind your work slip 1 purlwise, *knit 3, with the working yarn behind your work slip 1 purlwise* repeat from * to * until the end of the row before the edge stitch, knit 1.

Row 2: Purl 1, with the working yarn in front of the stitch slip 1 purlwise, *purl 3, with the working yarn in front of your work, slip 1 purlwise* repeat from * to * until the end of the row before the edge stitch, purl 1.

Row 3: *Knit 3, with the working yarn behind your work slip 1 purlwise* repeat from * to * until the end of the row before the edge stitch, knit 3.

Row 4: *Purl 3, with the working yarn in front of your work slip 1 purlwise* repeat from * to * until the end of the row before the edge stitch, purl 3.

Repeat rows: 1-4.

Bind off as follows: slip the edge stitch onto the right needle, knit 1, then insert the left needle through the slipped edge stitch from left to right and pass it over the knitted stitch; *now there is 1 stitch on the right needle; knit the next 1, then insert the left needle through the 1st stitch on the right needle from left to right and pass it over the 2nd stitch* repeat from * to * until the end of the row.

Pattern 34

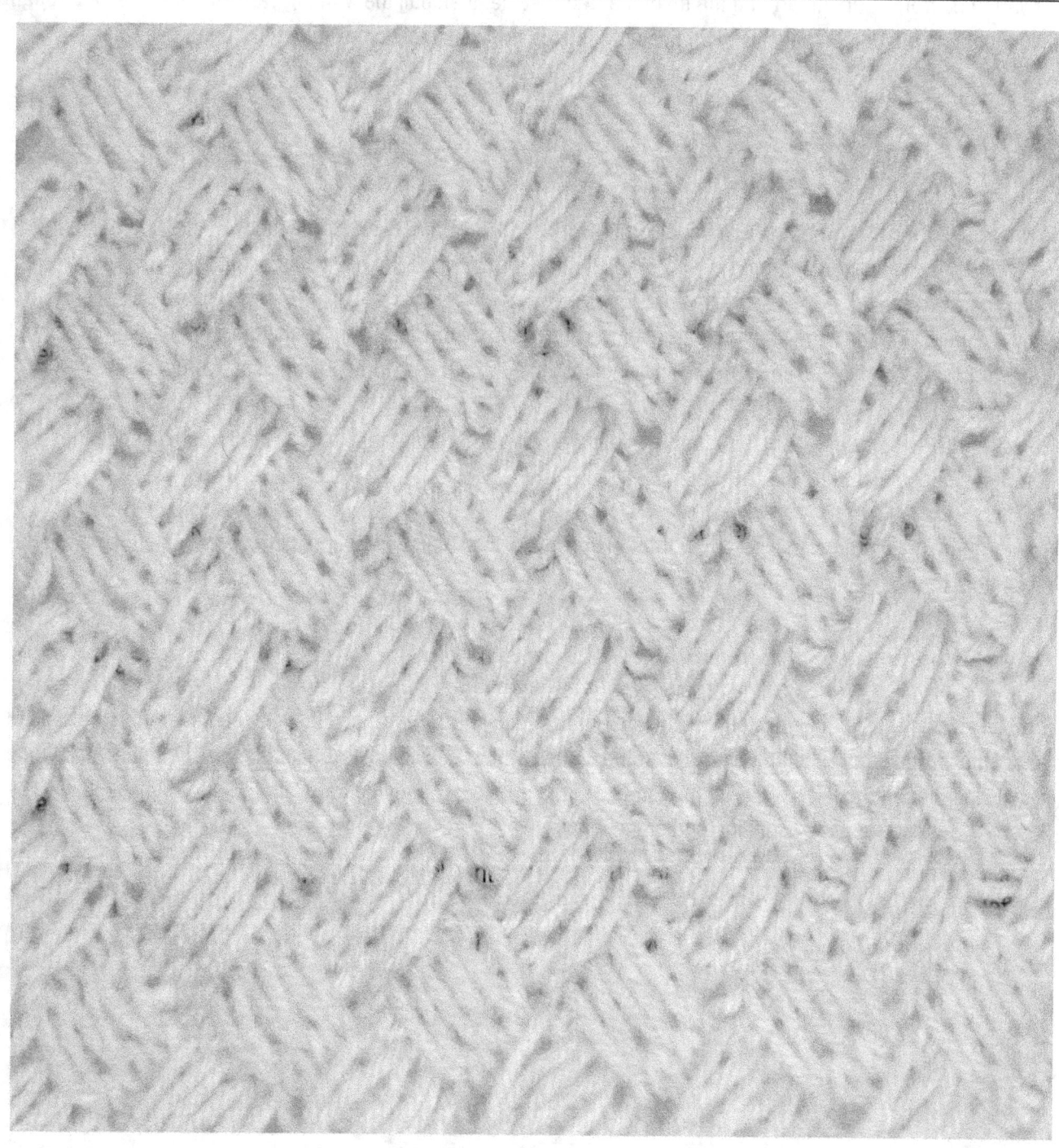

Cast on a multiple of 6, plus 2 edge stitches. Six-stitch repeat. Repeat rows: 1-4. **Needles: U.S. no. 7 (4.5 mm). Knit through the back leg, purl as follows:** with the working yarn in front of the stitch, insert the right needle through the stitch from back to front, move the working yarn under the right needle, and pull it with the needle through the stitch. The purl stitch that is worked this way sets up the knit stitch to be knitted through the back leg.

Description:

Row 2 (Back Side): Purl the edge stitch, *double yarn over forward (i.e., from yourself), purl 1* repeat from * to * until the end of the row, purl the edge stitch.

Row 2 (Front Side): Slip the edge stitch, slip each knit stitch purlwise from the left needle to the right one and slip each double yarn over off the left needle, leaving it as is, thus creating and moving elongated knit stitches onto the right needle, leave the last edge stitch on the left needle (now the working yarn is at the end of the right needle); *intersect 6 stitches with a slant to the right as follows: counting from left to right, insert the left needle through the 4th, 5th, and 6th stitches purlwise behind your work and slip all 6 stitches off the right needle, then pick up the 1st, 2nd, and 3rd stitches onto the right needle purlwise and slip them onto the left needle, now these 6 stitches are intersected on the left needle with a slant to the right* repeat from * to * until the end of the row, thus moving all the stitches from the right needle to the left one. Now knit all the stitches, including the edge stitches.

Row 3 (Back Side): Purl the first edge stitch, *double yarn over forward (i.e., from yourself), purl 1* repeat from * to * until the end of the row, purl the last edge stitch.

Row 4 (Front Side): Slip the edge stitch onto the right needle, slip each knit stitch from the left needle to the right one and slip each double yarn over off the left needle, leaving it as is, thus creating and moving elongated stitches onto the right needle; leave the last edge stitch on the left needle (now the working yarn is at the end of the right needle); slip the first 3 stitches from the right needle to the left one, *intersect 6 stitches with a slant to the left as follows: counting from left to right, insert the left needle through the 4th, 5th, and 6th stitches in front of your work and slip all 6 stitches off the right needle, then pick up the first 3 stitches onto the right needle purlwise behind your work and slip them onto the left needle; now these 6 stitches are intersected with a slant to the left* repeat from * to * until the end of the row, slip the last 3 stitches and the edge stitch onto the left needle. Now knit all the stitches tightly, including the edge stitches.

Repeat rows: 1-4.

Bind off as follows: After the last row 4, turn your work over. The Back Side: slip all the stitches from the left needle to the right one; thus, the working yarn is at the end of the right needle; turn your work over. The Front Side: slip 2 purlwise from the left needle to the right one, insert the left needle through the front leg of the 1st slipped stitch from left to right and pass it over the 2nd stitch (now there is 1 stitch on the right needle); *slip 1 purlwise from the left needle to the right one, insert the left needle through the front leg of the 1st stitch on the right needle from left to right and pass it over the 2nd stitch, now there is 1 stitch on the right needle* repeat from * to * until the end of the row.

Note: For trimming, bind off using larger needles than the working ones, as this method of binding off stitches creates a tight chain of stitches.

Pattern 35

Cast on a multiple of 4. **Knit without the edge stitches.** Four-stitch repeat. Repeat rows: 3-11. **Knit through the back leg, purl as follows:** with the working yarn in front of the stitch, insert the right needle through the stitch from back to front, move the working yarn under the needle, and pull it with the needle through the stitch. The purl stitch that is worked this way sets up the knit stitch to be knitted through the back leg.

Note: This pattern knits differently: the width knits vertically (i.e., knit the required width vertically, then turn your work horizontally). Cast on the number of stitches required for the height of your knitting. **Knit tightly. Needles: U.S. no. 4 (3.5 mm).**

Description:

Row 1: Slip 1, knit all the stitches.

Row 2: Slip 1, purl all the stitches.

Row 3: Knit 8 stitches as follows: *slip 1 purlwise, knit 7, then, leaving the rest of the stitches on the left needle, turn your work over to the Back Side. **The Back Side:** slip 1 purlwise, purl 7, then turn your work over to the Front Side* repeat from * to * 6 more times (i.e., 12 rows). **The Front Side:** slip 1, knit 11, then, leaving the rest of the stitches on the left needle, turn your work over to the Back Side. **The Back Side:** slip 1, purl 7, then, leaving 4 stitches on the left needle, turn your work over to the Front Side. **The Front Side:** ***slip 1, knit 7, then turn your work over to the Back Side. **The Back Side:** slip 1, purl 7, then turn your work over to the Front Side* repeat from *** to * 5 more time (i.e., 10 rows), then—**on the Front Side**—slip 1, knit 11, then turn your work over to the Back Side. **The Back Side:** slip 1, purl 7, then, leaving 4 more stitches on the left needle, turn your work over to the Front Side*** repeat from *** to *** until the end of the row, until the last 8 stitches on the Front Side. **The Front Side.** Knit the last 8 stitches as follows: ****slip 1, knit 7, then turn your work over to the Back Side. **The Back Side:** slip 1, purl 7**** repeat from **** to **** 5 more times (i.e., 10 rows). **Note:** After the last turn over, purl all the stitches until the end of the row, connecting the separate stitches in this row.

Row 4 (Front Side): Slip 1, knit all the stitches tightly.

Row 5 (Back Side): Slip 1, purl all the stitches tightly.

Row 6 (Front Side): Slip 1, knit all the stitches tightly.

Row 7 (Back Side): Note: From row 7, begin knitting on the Back Side as follows: *slip 1, purl 7, then, leaving the rest of the stitches on the left needle, turn your work over to the Front Side. **The Front Side:** slip 1, knit 7, then turn your work over to the Back Side* repeat from * to * 6 more times (i.e., 12 rows), then—**on the Back Side**—slip 1, purl 11, then, leaving the rest of the stitches on the left needle, turn your work over to the Front Side. **The Front Side:** slip 1, knit 7, then, leaving 4 stitches on the left needle, turn your work over to the Back Side. **The Back Side:** ***slip 1, purl 7, then turn your work over to the Front Side. **The Front Side:** slip 1, knit 7, then turn your work over to the Back Side* repeat from *** to * 5 more times (i.e., 10 rows), then—**on the Back Side**—slip 1, purl 11, then turn your work over to the Front Side. **The Front Side:** slip 1, knit 7, then, leaving 4 more stitches on the left needle, turn your work over to the Back Side*** Repeat from *** to *** until the end of the row, until the last 8 stitches on the Back Side. Purl the last 8 stitches as follows: ****slip 1, purl 7, then turn your work over to the Front Side. **The Front Side:** slip 1, knit 7, then turn your work over to the Back Side**** repeat from **** to **** 4 more times (i.e., 8 rows). **The Back Side:** slip 1, purl 7, then turn your work over to the Front Side.

Row 8 (Front Side): Slip 1, knit all the stitches, connecting the separate stitches in this row.

Row 9 (Back Side): Slip 1, purl all the stitches.

Row 10 (Front Side): Slip 1, knit all the stitches.

Row 11 (Back Side): Slip 1, purl all the stitches.

Repeat rows: 3-11.

Note: At the end of your work, **bind off in the last row 10, for symmetry with rows 1-2.**

Bind off as follows: *knit 2 together through the back legs, then slip the received stitch from the right needle to the left one* repeat from * to * until the end of the row.

Pattern 36

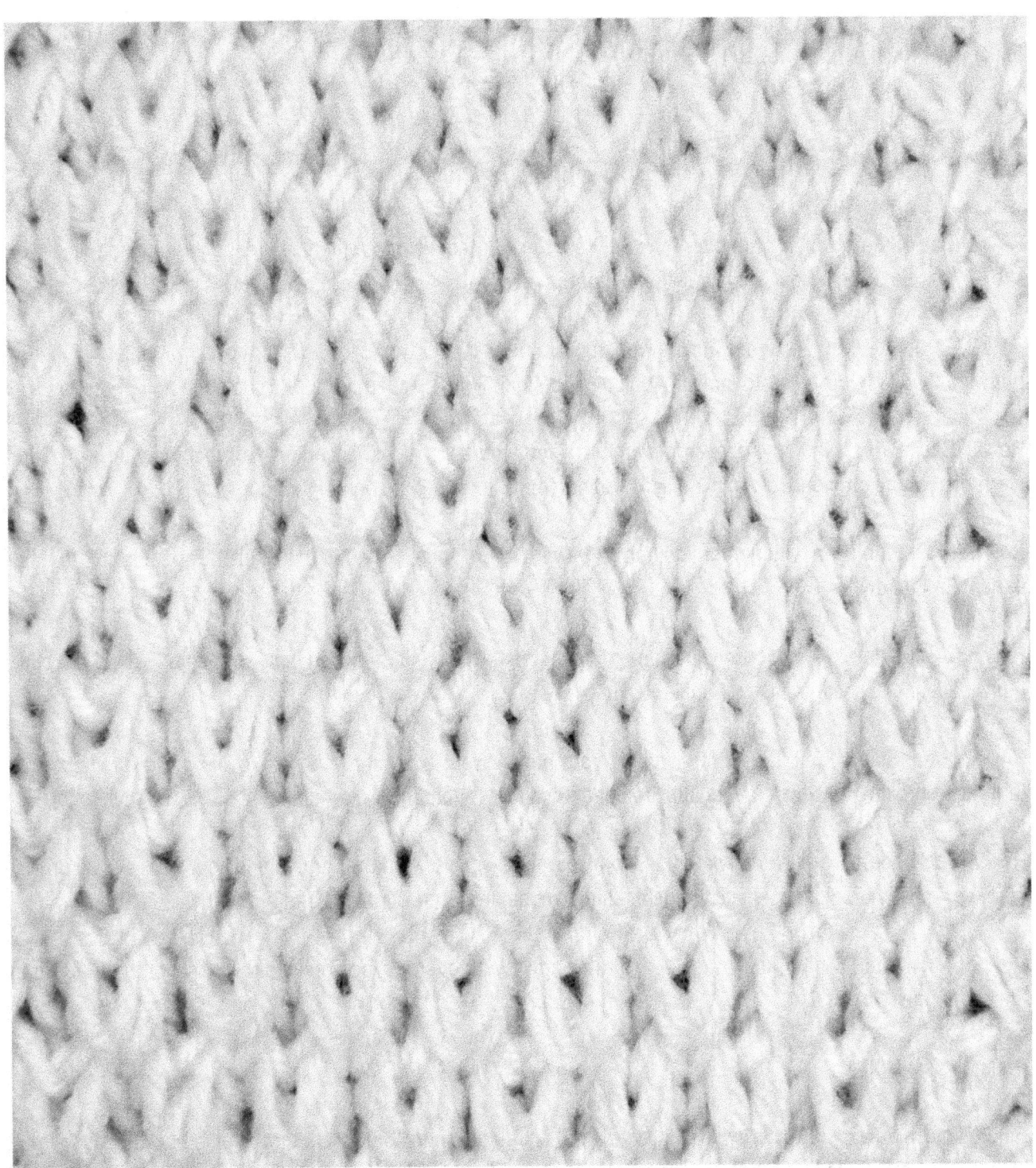

Cast on a multiple of 2, plus 2 edge stitches. Two-stitch repeat. Repeat rows: 1-8.The edge stitches are not included in the description below and must be added. Slip the first edge stitch; purl the last edge stitch as if to

purl in knitting through the back leg as follows: insert the right needle through the stitch from back to front, move the working yarn under the right needle, and pull it with the needle through the stitch.

Knit through the front leg; purl as follows: with the working yarn in front of the stitch, wrap the working yarn forward (i.e., from yourself) around the tip of the right needle, then pull the working yarn with the needle through the stitch. The purl stitch that is worked this way sets up the knit stitch to be knitted through the front leg. **Use a bulky yarn. Needles: U.S. no. 10 (5.75 mm).**

Description:

Row 1 (Back Side): *Knit 1, yarn over forward (i.e., from yourself) **twice**, with the working yarn behind your work slip 1 purlwise* repeat from * to * until the end of the row.

Row 2 (Front Side): *Knit 1, then with the working yarn behind your work, slip 1 (2 yarn overs of the previous row) purlwise, unrolling the 2 yarn overs into 1 elongated stitch, knit 1* repeat from * to * until the end of the row.

Row 3 (Back Side): *Knit 1, yarn over forward (i.e., from yourself), with the working yarn behind your work slip 2 (yarn over of the previous row and 1 stitch)* repeat from * to * until the end of the row.

Row 4 (Front Side): *Knit 3 together (1 stitch and 2 yarn overs of the previous row), knit 1* repeat from * to * until the end of the row.

Row 5 (Back Side): *Yarn over forward (i.e., from yourself) **twice**, with the working yarn behind your work slip 1 purlwise, knit 1* repeat from * to * until the end of the row.

Row 6 (Front Side): *Knit 2, with the working yarn behind your work slip 1 (2 yarn overs of the previous row) purlwise, unrolling the 2 yarn overs into 1 elongated stitch* repeat from * to * until the end of the row.

Row 7 (Back Side): *Yarn over forward (i.e., from yourself), with the working yarn behind your work slip 2 purlwise (yarn over of the previous row and 1 stitch), knit 1* repeat from * to * until the end of the row.

Row 8 (Front Side): *Knit 1, knit 3 together (1 stitch and 2 yarn overs of the previous row)* repeat from * to * until the end of the row.

Repeat rows: 1-8.

Bind off purlwise after the last row 8 as follows: *purl 2 together (purl as if to knit through the back leg as follows: insert the right needle through the stitch from back to front, move the working yarn under the right needle, and pull it through the stitch), slip the received stitch from the right needle to the left one* repeat from * to * until the end of the row.

Pattern 37
Reversible Double knitting

Cast on a multiple of 2, plus 2 edge stitches. Two-stitch repeat. Repeat row 1. The edge stitches are not included in the description below and must be added. Slip the first edge stitch purlwise; **knit the last edge stitch through**

the front leg.

Note: Out of each 2 knitted rows, 1 row shows on the Front Side and 1 row shows on the Back Side, creating a double fabric.

Description:

Row 1: *Knit 1 through the front leg, then with the working yarn in front of your work, slip 1 purlwise* repeat from * to * until the end of the row, **knit the edge stitch through the front leg.**

Repeat row 1.

Bind off every 2 stitches as 1 stitch as follows: *insert the right needle through the 1st knit stitch and then through the edge stitch and knit them together through the front legs; *now there is 1 stitch on the right needle; knit the next 2 together through the front legs, (1 stitch of the front side and 1 stitch of the backside); now there are 2 stitches on the right needle; insert the left needle through the 1st stitch on the right needle from left to right and pass it over the 2nd stitch* repeat from * to * until the end of the row.

Pattern 38

Cast on a multiple of 2, plus 1 for symmetry and 2 edge stitches. Two-stitch repeat. Repeat rows: 1-4. The edge stitches are not included in the description below and must be added. Slip the first edge stitch; purl the last edge stitch.

Knit through the back leg, purl as follows: with the working yarn in front of the stitch, insert the right needle through the stitch from back to front, move the working yarn under the needle, and pull it with the needle through the stitch. The purl stitch that is worked this way sets up the knit stitch to be knitted through the back leg. **Use a bulky yarn.**

Description:

Row 1: *Purl 1, knit 1 as follows: insert the right needle through the back leg and wrap the working yarn forward (i.e., from yourself) around the tip of the right needle 2 times, then finish the stitch, as usual* repeat from * to * until the end of the row before the edge stitch, purl 1.

Row 2: *Knit 1, then with the working yarn in front of your work, slip the next 1 purlwise, simultaneously unrolling the loops, receiving 1 elongated stitch* repeat from * to * until the end of the row before the edge stitch, knit 1.

Row 3: *Purl 1, then with the working yarn behind your work, slip 1 (1 elongated stitch) purlwise* repeat from * to * until the end of the row before the edge stitch, purl 1.

Row 4: *Knit 1, then with the working yarn in front of your work, slip 1 (1 elongated stitch) purlwise* repeat from * to * until the end of the row before the edge stitch, knit 1.

Repeat rows: 1-4.

Bind off after the last row 4 as follows: slip the edge stitch onto the right needle, knit 1, then insert the left needle through the slipped stitch from left to right and pass it over the knitted stitch; *now there is 1 stitch on the right needle; knit the next 1, then insert the left needle through the 1st stitch on the right needle from left to right and pass it over the 2nd stitch* repeat from * to * until the end of the row.

Pattern 39

Cast on a multiple of 2 stitches, plus 1 stitch for symmetry and 2 edge stitches. Two-stitch repeat. Repeat rows: 1-4. The edge stitches are not included in the description below and must be added. Slip the first edge stitch; purl the last edge stitch.

Knit through the back leg, purl as follows: with the working yarn in front of the stitch, insert the right needle through the stitch from back to front, move the working yarn under the needle, and pull it with the needle through the stitch. The purl stitch that is worked this way sets up the knit stitch to be knitted through the back leg. **Use a bulky yarn.**

Description:

Row 1: *Purl 1, knit 1 as follows: insert the right needle through the stitch from left to right and wrap the working yarn forward (i.e., from yourself) around the tip of the right needle 3 times, then finish the stitch, as usual* repeat from * to * until the end of the row before the edge stitch, purl 1.

Row 2: *Knit 1, then with the working yarn in front of your work, slip the next 1 purlwise, simultaneously unrolling this stitch into 1 elongated stitch* repeat from * to * until the end of the row before the edge stitch, knit 1.

Row 3: *Purl 1, with the working yarn behind your work slip 1 purlwise* repeat from * to * until the end of the row before the edge stitch, purl 1.

Row 4: *Knit 1, with the working yarn in front of your work slip 1 elongated stitch purlwise* repeat from * to * until the end of the row before the edge stitch, knit 1.

Repeat rows: 1-4.

Bind off after the last row 4 as follows: slip the edge stitch onto the right needle, knit 1, then insert the left needle through the slipped stitch from left to right and pass it over the knitted stitch; *now there is 1 stitch on the right needle; knit the next 1, then insert the left needle through the 1st stitch on the right needle from left to right and pass it over the 2nd stitch* repeat from * to * until the end of the row.

Pattern 40

Cast on a multiple of 3, plus 1 for symmetry and 2 edge stitches. Three-stitch repeat. Repeat rows: 1-4. The edge stitches are not included in the description below and must be added. **Knit the first edge stitch through the front**

leg; **knit the last edge stitch through the front leg. Knit through the front leg; purl as follows:** with the working yarn in front of the stitch, insert the right needle through the stitch from back to front, wrap the working yarn forward (i.e., from yourself) around the tip of the right needle, then pull the working yarn with the right needle through the stitch. The purl stitch that is worked this way sets up the knit stitch to be knitted through the front leg.

Description:

Row 1: Knit all the stitches.

Row 2: *Knit 1, with the working yarn behind your work slip 2* repeat from * to * until the end of the row before the edge stitch, knit 1.

Row 3: *Knit 1, purl 2* repeat from * to * until the end of the row before the edge stitch, knit 1.

Row 4: *With the working yarn in front of your work, slip 1, knit the next 2* repeat from * to * until the end of the row before the edge stitch, with the working yarn in front of the work slip 1.

Repeat rows: 1-4.

Bind off as follows: after the last row 4, turn your work over. The Front Side: slip all the stitches from the left needle to the right one; thus, the working yarn is at the end of the right needle, then turn your work over. The Back Side: slip 2 purlwise from the left needle to the right one, insert the left needle through the front leg of the 1st slipped stitch from left to right, and pass it over the 2nd stitch (now there is 1 stitch on the right needle); *slip 1 purlwise from the left needle to the right one, insert the left needle through the front leg of the 1st stitch on the right needle from left to right and pass it over the 2nd stitch, now there is 1 stitch on the right needle* repeat from * to * until the end of the row.

Note: For trimming, bind off using larger needles than the working ones as this method of binding off creates a tight chain of stitches.

Pattern 41

Cast on a multiple of 8, plus 2, plus 2 edge stitches. Eight-stitch repeat. Repeat rows: 3-14. The edge stitches are not included in the description below and must be added. Slip the first edge stitch; purl the last edge stitch

as if to purl in knitting through the back leg as follows: insert the right needle through the stitch from back to front, move the working yarn under the right needle, and pull it with the needle through the stitch.

Knit through the back leg, purl as follows: with the working yarn in front of the stitch, insert the right needle through the stitch from back to front, move the working yarn under the right needle, and pull it with the needle through the stitch. The purl stitch that is worked this way sets up the knit stitch to be knitted through the back leg.

Description:

Row 1 (set up row): Knit all the stitches.

Row 2 (set up row): Purl all the stitches.

Row 3: Knit 1, *with the working yarn in front of your work slip 4 purlwise, knit the next 4* repeat from * to * until the end of the row before the edge stitch, with the working yarn in front of your work slip 1 purlwise.

Row 4: *Purl 4, then with the working yarn behind your work, slip the next 4 purlwise* repeat from * to * until the end of the row before the edge stitch, purl 2.

Row 5: Knit 3, *with the working yarn in front of your work slip 4 purlwise, knit the next 4* repeat from * to * until the end of the row before the edge stitch, with the working yarn in front of your work slip 4 purlwise, knit 3.

Row 6: Purl 2, *with the working yarn behind your work slip 4 purlwise, purl the next 4* repeat from * to * until the end of the row.

Row 7: With the working yarn in front of your work, slip 1 purlwise, *knit 4, with the working yarn in front of your work slip the next 4* repeat from * to * until the end of the row before the edge stitch, knit 1.

Row 8: *With the working yarn behind your work, slip 4 purlwise, purl the next 4* repeat from * to * until the end of the row before the edge stitch, with the working yarn behind your work slip 2 purlwise.

Row 9: Knit 2, *With the working yarn in front of your work slip 4 purlwise, knit the next 4* repeat from * to * until the end of the row.

Row 10: With the working yarn behind your work, slip 1 purlwise, *purl 4, then with the working yarn behind your work, slip the next 4 purlwise* repeat from * to * until the end of the row before the edge stitch, purl 1.

Row 11: *With the working yarn in front of your work, slip 1 purlwise, knit the next 4* repeat from * to * until the end of the row before the edge stitch, with the working yarn in front of your work slip 2 purlwise.

Row 12: With the working yarn behind your work, slip 3 purlwise, *purl 4, with the working yarn behind your work, slip the next 4 purlwise* repeat from * to * until the end of the row before the edge stitch, purl 4, with the working yarn behind your work slip 3 purlwise.

Row 13: With the working yarn in front of your work, slip 2 purlwise, *knit 4, with the working yarn in front of your work slip the next 4 purlwise* repeat from * to * until the end of the row.

Row 14: Purl 1, *with the working yarn behind your work slip 4 purlwise, purl the next 4* repeat from * to * until the end of the row before the edge stitch, with the working yarn behind your work slip 1 purlwise.

Repeat rows: 3-14.

Bind off after the last row 14 as follows: slip the edge stitch onto the right needle, knit 1, then insert the left needle through the slipped stitch from left to right and pass it over the knitted stitch; *now there is 1 stitch on the right needle; knit the next 1, insert the left needle through the 1st stitch on the right needle from left to right and pass it over the 2nd stitch* repeat from * to * until the end of the row.

Pattern 42

Cast on a multiple of 4, plus 1, plus 2 edge stitches. Four-stitch repeat. Repeat rows: 1-12. The edge stitches are not included in the description below and must be added. Slip the first edge stitch; purl the last edge stitch. **Knit through the back leg, purl as follows:** with the working yarn in front of the stitch, insert the right needle through the stitch from back to front, move the working yarn under the needle, and pull it with the needle through the stitch. The purl stitch that is worked this way sets up the knit stitch to be knitted through the back leg. **Knit tightly.**

Description:

Row 1: Knit all the stitches.

Row 2: Purl all the stitches.

Row 3: Knit all the stitches.

Row 4: Purl all the stitches.

Row 5: Knit 2, *slip 1 off the left needle and slip it down—4 rows, then pick up this stitch with the received 4 horizontal loops above this stitch onto the left needle and knit 5 together (1 stitch and 4 horizontal loops), then knit the next 3* repeat from * to * until the end of the row before the edge stitch, the last 3 stitches knit as follows: slip 1 stitch off the left needle and slip it down—4 rows, then pick up this stitch with the received 4 horizontal loops above this stitch onto the left needle and knit 5 together (1 stitch and 4 horizontal loops), then knit 2.

Row 6: Purl all the stitches.

Row 7: Knit all the stitches.

Row 8: Purl all the stitches.

Row 9: Knit all the stitches.

Row 10: Purl all the stitches.

Row 11: *Slip 1 off the left needle and slip it down—4 rows, then pick up this stitch with the received 4 horizontal loops above this stitch onto the left needle and knit 5 together (1 stitch and 4 horizontal loops), then knit the next 3* repeat from * to * until the end of the row before the edge stitch, slip the last 1 stitch off the left needle and slip it down—4 rows, then pick up this stitch with the received 4 horizontal loops above this stitch onto the left needle and knit 5 together (1 stitch and 4 horizontal loops).

Row 12: Purl all the stitches.

Repeat rows: 1-12.

Bind off after the last row 12 as follows: slip the edge stitch onto the right needle, knit 1, then insert the left needle through the slipped stitch from left to right and pass it over the knitted stitch; *now there is 1 stitch on the right needle; knit the next 1, then insert the left needle through the 1st stitch on the right needle from left to right and pass it over the 2nd stitch* repeat from * to * until the end of the row.

Pattern 43

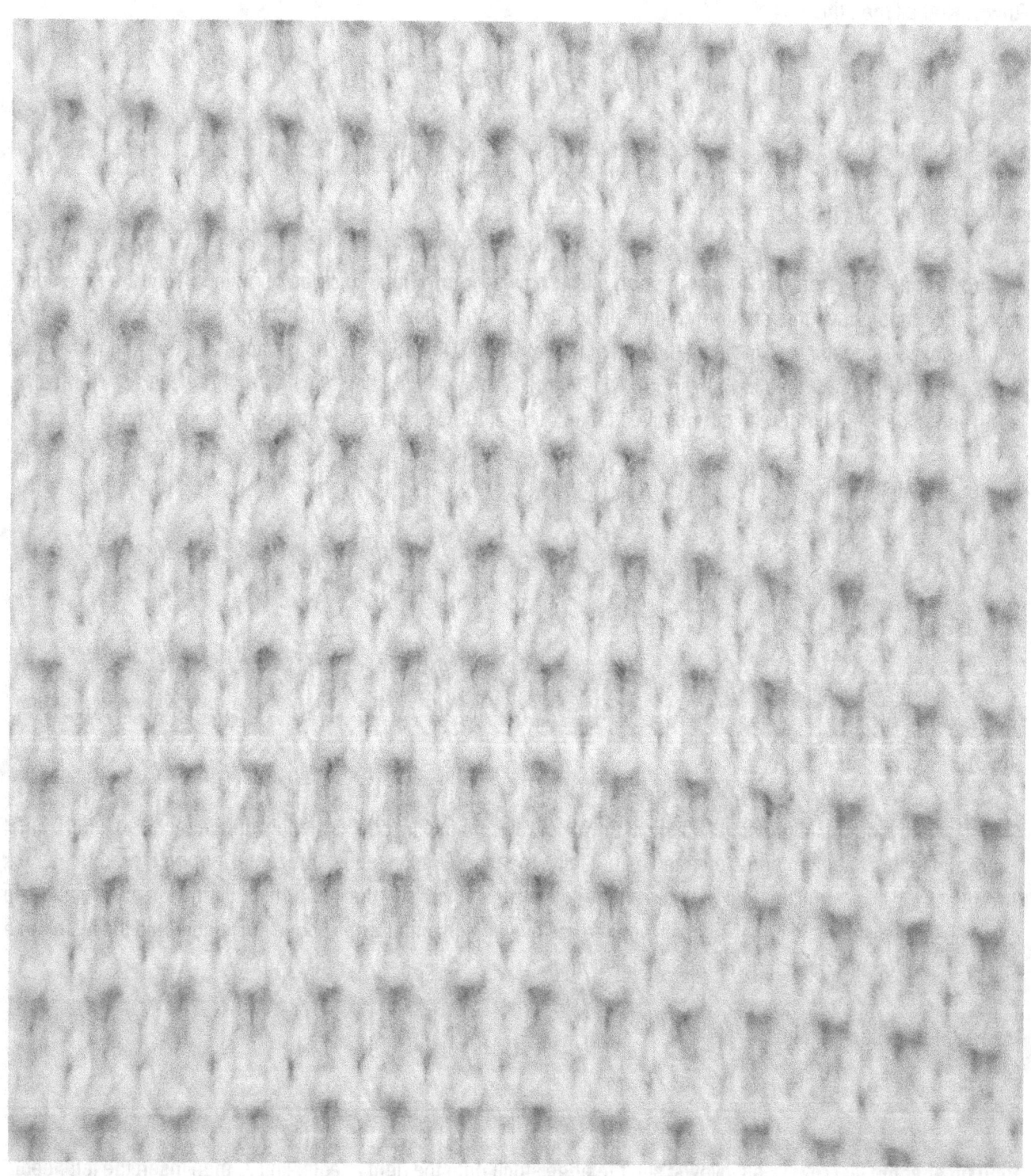

Cast on a multiple of 2, plus 2 edge stitches. Two-stitch repeat. Repeat rows: 1-4. The edge stitches are not included in the description below and must be added. **Knit the first edge stitch through the front leg; purl the last edge stitch.**

Purl all stitches as if to purl in knitting through the back leg as follows: with the working yarn in front of the stitch, insert the right needle through the stitch from back to front, move the working yarn under the right needle, and pull it with the needle through the stitch. The purl stitch that is worked this way sets up the knit stitch to be knitted through the back leg.

Description:

Row 1: *Knit 1 through the back leg, with the working yarn behind your work slip 1 purlwise* repeat from * to * until the end of the row.

Row 2: *With the working yarn in front of your work, slip 1 purlwise, knit 1 through the front leg* repeat from * to * until the end of the row.

Row 3: *Knit 1 through the front leg, knit 1 through the back leg* repeat from * to * until the end of the row.

Row 4: Purl all the stitches.

Repeat rows: 1-4.

Bind off as follows: after the last row 3, turn your work over; the Back Side: slip all the stitches from the left needle to the right one; thus, the working yarn is at the end of the row; turn your work over; the Front Side: slip 2 stitches from the left needle to the right one, insert the left needle through the 1st slipped stitch from left to right and pass it over the 2nd stitch; now there is 1 stitch on the right needle; *slip 1 from the left needle to the right one, insert the left needle through the 1st stitch on the right needle from left to right and pass it over the 2nd stitch; now there is 1 stitch on the right needle* repeat from * to * until the end of the row.

Note: Bind off using larger needles than the working ones to create a larger chain of edge stitches for trimming, as this method of binding off stitches creates a tight chain of edge stitches.

Pattern 44

Cast on a multiple of 2, plus 1, and 2 edge stitches. Two-stitch repeat. Repeat rows: 1-12. The edge stitches are not included in the description below and must be added. Slip the first edge stitch; purl the last edge stitch as if

to purl in knitting through the back leg as follows: insert the right needle through the stitch from back to front, move the working yarn under the right needle, and pull it with the needle through the stitch.

Knit through the front leg; purl as follows: with the working yarn in front of the stitch, wrap the working yarn forward (i.e., from yourself) around the tip of the right needle, then pull the working yarn with the needle through the stitch. The purl stitch that is worked this way sets up the knit stitch to be knitted through the front leg.

Description:

Row 1 (Back Side): *Purl 1, with the working yarn behind your work slip 1 purlwise* repeat from * to * until the end of the row before the edge stitch, purl 1.

Row 2 (Front Side): Knit 1, *purl 1, knit 1* repeat from * to * until the end of the row.

Row 3 (Back Side): *Purl 1, knit 1* repeat from * to * until the end of the row before the edge stitch, purl 1.

Row 4 (Front Side): Knit 1, *purl 1, knit 1* repeat from * to * until the end of the row.

Row 5 (Back Side): *Purl 1, knit 1 * repeat from * to * until the end of the row before the edge stitch, purl 1.

Row 6 (Front Side): Knit 1, *insert the left needle from left to right through the slipped stitch 4 rows below and move it onto the right needle, knit the next 1, then insert the left needle through the slipped stitch on the right needle from left to right and pass it over the knitted one, knit the next 1* repeat from * to * until the end of the row.

Row 7 (Back Side): With the working yarn behind your work, slip 1 purlwise, purl the next 1* repeat from * to * until the end of the row before the edge stitch, with the working yarn behind your work slip 1.

Row 8 (Front Side): Purl 1, *knit 1, purl 1* repeat from * to * until the end of the row.

Row 9 (Back Side): *Knit 1, purl 1* repeat from * to * until the end of the row before the edge stitch, knit 1.

Row 10 (Front Side): *Purl 1, *knit 1, purl 1 * repeat from * to * until the end of the row.

Row 11 (Back Side): *Knit 1, purl 1 * repeat from * to * until the end of the row before the edge stitch, knit 1.

Row 12 (Front Side): *Insert the left needle from left to right through the slipped stitch 4 rows below and move it onto the right needle, knit the next 1, then insert the left needle through the slipped stitch on the right needle from left to right and pass it over the knitted one, knit the next 1* repeat from * to * until the end of the row before the edge stitch, insert the left needle from left to right through the slipped stitch 4 rows below and move it onto the right needle, knit the next 1, then insert the left needle through the slipped stitch on the right needle from left to right and pass it over the knitted one.

Repeat rows: 1-12.

Bind off after the last row 12 as follows: Slip 1 stitch from the left needle to the right one, purl the next 1 as if to purl in knitting through the back leg (i.e., insert the right needle through the stitch from back to front, move the working yarn under the right needle, and pull it with the needle through the stitch), then insert the left needle through the slipped stitch from left to right, and pass it over the purled one (now there is 1 stitch on the right needle), *purl 1 as if to purl in knitting through the back leg, then insert the left needle through the stitch on the right needle from left to right and pass it over the purled one (now there is 1 stitch on the right needle)* repeat from * to * until the end of the row.

Pattern 45

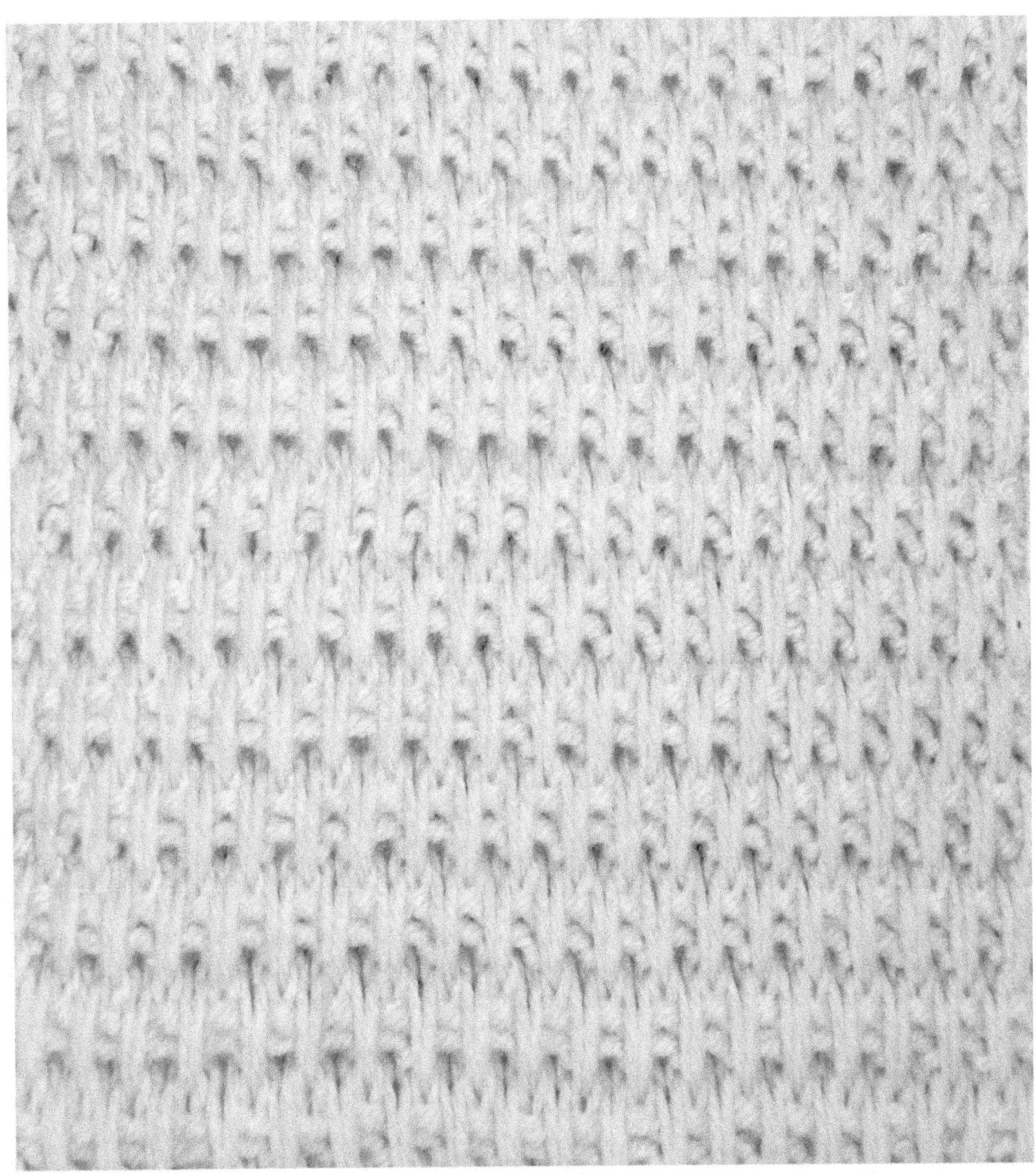

Cast on a multiple of 2, plus 2 edge stitches. Two-stitch repeat. Repeat rows: 1-8. The edge stitches are not included in the description below and must be added. Slip the first edge stitch; purl the last edge stitch as if to

purl in knitting through the back leg as follows: insert the right needle through the stitch from back to front, move the working yarn under the right needle, and pull it with the needle through the stitch.

Description:

Row 1: *Yarn over forward (i.e., from yourself) **twice**, knit 2* repeat from * to * until the end of the row.

Row 2: *Knit 1, then with the working yarn in front of your work, slip 1 purlwise onto the right needle, then slip 2 yarn overs of the previous row off the needle and leave them as they are* repeat from * to * until the end of the row.

Row 3: *With the working yarn behind your work, slip 1 purlwise, knit 1* repeat from * to * until the end of the row.

Row 4: *Knit 1, with the working yarn in front of your work slip 1 purlwise* repeat from * to * until the end of the row.

Row 5: *Knit 1, yarn over forward (i.e., from yourself) **twice**, knit 1* repeat from * to * until the end of the row.

Row 6: *With the working yarn in front of your work, slip 1 purlwise onto the right needle, then slip 2 yarn overs of the previous row off the left needle and leave them as they are, then knit 1* repeat from * to * until the end of the row.

Row 7: *Knit 1, then with the working yarn behind your work, slip 1 purlwise* repeat from * to * until the end of the row.

Row 8: *With the working yarn in front of your work, slip 1 purlwise, knit 1* repeat from * to * until the end of the row.

Repeat rows: 1-8.

Bind off after the last row 8 as follows: slip the edge stitch onto the right needle, knit 1, then insert the left needle through the slipped edge stitch from left to right and pass it over the knitted stitch; *now there is 1 stitch on the right needle; knit the next 1, insert the left needle through the 1st stitch from left to right and pass it over the 2nd stitch* repeat from * to * until the end of the row.

Pattern 46

Cast on a multiple of 4, plus 3, plus 2 edge stitches. Four-stitch repeat. Repeat rows: 1-8. The edge stitches are not included in the description below and must be added. Slip the first edge stitch; purl the last edge stitch as if

to purl in knitting through the back leg as follows: insert the right needle through the stitch from back to front, move the working yarn under the right needle, and pull it with the needle through the stitch.

Knit through the front leg; purl as follows: with the working yarn in front of the stitch, wrap the working yarn forward (i.e., from yourself) around the tip of the right needle, then pull the working yarn through the stitch. The purl stitch that is worked this way sets up the knit stitch to be knitted through the front leg. **Needles: U.S. no. 7 (4.5 mm). Use a bulky yarn.**

Description:

Row 1: *Purl 1, knit 1, purl 1, knit 1* repeat from * to * until the end of the row before the edge stitch, the last 3 stitches, purl 1, knit 1, purl 1.

Row 2: Knit 1, purl 1, knit 1, *purl 1, knit 1, purl 1, knit 1* repeat from * to * until the end of the row.

Row 3: *Knit 1, purl 1, knit 1, then with the working yarn behind your work, slip 1 purlwise* repeat from * to * until the end of the row before the edge stitch, the last 3 stitches, knit 1, purl 1, knit 1.

Row 4: Purl 1, knit 1, purl 1, *with the working yarn in front of your work slip, 1 purlwise, purl 1, knit 1, purl 1* repeat from * to * until the end of the row.

Row 5: *purl 1, knit 1, purl 1, knit 1* repeat from * to * until the end of the row before the edge stitch, the last 3 stitches, purl 1, knit 1, purl 1.

Row 6: Knit 1, purl 1, knit 1, *purl 1, knit 1, purl 1, knit 1* repeat from * to * until the end of the row.

Row 7: *Knit 1, with the working yarn behind your work slip 1 purlwise, knit 1, purl 1* repeat from * to * until the end of the row before the edge stitch, the last 3 stitches, knit 1, with the working yarn behind your work slip 1 purlwise, knit 1.

Row 8: Purl 1, with the working yarn in front of your work slip 1 purlwise, purl 1, *knit 1, purl 1, with the working yarn in front of your work slip 1 purlwise, purl 1* repeat from * to * until the end of the row.

Repeat rows: 1-8.

Bind off after the last row 8 as follows: slip the edge stitch onto the right needle, knit 1, then pass the edge stitch over the knitted stitch; *now there is 1 stitch on the right needle; knit the next 1, insert the left needle through the 1st stitch from left to right and pass it over the 2nd stitch* repeat from * to * until the end of the row.

Pattern 47

Cast on any number of stitches. Repeat rows: 1-16. Knit the first edge stitch; purl the last edge stitch as if to purl in knitting through the back leg as follows: insert the right needle through the stitch from back to front, move the working yarn under the right needle, and pull it with the needle through the stitch.

Knit through the front leg, purl as follows: with the working yarn in front of the stitch, wrap the working yarn forward (i.e., from yourself) around the tip of the right needle, then pull the working yarn with the needle through the stitch. The purl stitch that is worked this way sets up the knit stitch to be knitted through the front leg.

Note: For creating folds, temporary mark the stitches, connecting a piece of contrasting colored yarn to the working yarn. Remove the helping pieces of yarn after the folds are made.

Description:

Row 1: Connect a piece of contrasting colored yarn to the working yarn and knit all the stitches.

Row 2: Purl all the stitches.

Row 3: Knit all the stitches.

Row 4: Purl all the stitches.

Rows 5-12: Repeat rows 3-4.

Row 13: Knit all the stitches together with all marked stitches in row 1 as follows: pick up the marked stitches onto an additional needle, then *knit 1 together with the corresponding marked stitch* repeat from * to * until the end of the row.

Row 14: Purl all the stitches.

Row 15: Knit all the stitches.

Row 16: Purl all the stitches.

Repeat rows: 1-16.

Bind off after the last row 16 as follows: slip the edge stitch onto the right needle, knit 1, then insert the left needle through the slipped edge stitch from left to right and pass it over the knitted stitch *now there is 1 stitch on the right needle; knit the next 1, insert the left needle through the 1st stitch from left to right and pass it over the 2nd stitch* repeat from * to * until the end of the row.

Pattern 48

Cast on a multiple of 20, plus 2 edge stitches. Twenty-stitch repeat. Repeat rows: 1-28. The edge stitches are not included in the description below and must be added. Slip the first edge stitch; purl the last edge stitch as if to purl in knitting through the back leg as follows: insert the right needle through the stitch from back to front, move the working yarn under the right needle, and pull it with the needle through the stitch. **Knit through the front legs. Note:** For creating folds, temporary mark 4 stitches in certain rows and places as described below, connecting a piece of contrasting colored yarn to the working yarn. Remove the helping pieces of yarn after the folds are made.

Description:

Row 1: Knit 4, then *mark the next 4 for the future fold as follows: connect a piece of contrasting colored yarn to the working yarn and knit 4, then knit 16* repeat from * to * before the edge stitch, connect a piece of contrasting colored yarn to the working yarn and knit 4, thus marking these 4 stitches for the future fold, then knit the last 12.

Rows 2-12: Knit all the stitches.

Row 13: Knit 4, *knit 4 together with 4 marked stitches in row 1 as follows: pick up 4 corresponding marked stitches onto an additional needle, knit the 1st stitch together with the 1st corresponding marked stitch, knit the 2nd stitch together with the 2nd corresponding marked stitch, knit the 3rd stitch together with the 3rd corresponding marked stitch, knit the 4th stitch together with the 4th corresponding marked stitch, then knit 16* repeat from * to * before the edge stitch, knit 4 together with the 4 corresponding marked stitches as described in this row, then knit 12.

Row 14: Knit all the stitches.

Row 15: Knit 12, *connect a piece of contrasting colored yarn to the working yarn then knit 4, thus marking these 4 stitches for the future fold, then knit 16* repeat from * to * before the edge stitch, the last 8 stitches, knit as follows: connect a piece of contrasting colored yarn to the working yarn then knit 4, thus marking these 4 stitches for the future fold, then knit the last 4.

Rows 16-26: Knit all the stitches.

Row 27: Knit 12, *knit 4 together with the 4 corresponding marked stitches in row 15 as described in row 13, then knit 16* repeat from * to * until the end of the row before the edge stitch, the last 8 stitches, knit as follows: knit 4 together with the 4 corresponding marked stitches as described in row 13, then knit the last 4.

Row 28: Knit all the stitches.

Repeat rows: 1-28.

Bind off after the last row 28 as follows: slip the edge stitch onto the right needle, knit 1, then insert the left needle through the slipped edge stitch from left to right and pass it over the knitted stitch; *now there is 1 stitch on the right needle; knit the next 1; insert the left needle through the 1st stitch from left to right and pass it over the 2nd stitch* repeat from * to * until the end of the row.

Pattern 49

Cast on a multiple of 15, plus 2 edge stitches. Fifteen-stitch repeat. Repeat rows: 1-70. The edge stitches are not included in the description below and must be added. Slip the first edge stitch; purl the last edge stitch as if to

purl in knitting through the back leg as follows: insert the right needle through the stitch from back to front, move the working yarn under the right needle, and pull it with the needle through the stitch.

Knit through the front leg, purl as follows: with the working yarn in front of the stitch, wrap the working yarn forward (i.e., from yourself) around the tip of the right needle, then pull the working yarn with the needle through the stitch. The purl stitch that is worked this way sets up the knit stitch to be knitted through the front leg.

Note: For creating folds, temporary mark 3 stitches in certain rows and places as described below, connecting a piece of contrasting colored yarn to the working yarn. Remove the helping pieces of yarn after the folds are made.

Description:

Row 1: *Mark 3 stitches for the future fold as follows: connect a piece of contrasting colored yarn to the working yarn and knit 3, then knit the next 12* repeat from * to * until the end of the row.

Row 2: Purl all the stitches.

Row 3: Knit all the stitches.

Row 4: Purl all the stitches.

Rows 5-12: Alternate rows 3-4.

Row 13: *Knit 3 together with 3 marked stitches in row 1 as follows: pick up 3 corresponding marked stitches onto an additional needle, knit the 1st stitch together with the 1st marked stitch, knit the 2nd stitch together with the 2nd marked stitch, knit the 3rd stitch together with the 3rd marked stitch, then knit 12* repeat from * to * until the end of the row.

Row 14: Purl all the stitches.

Row 15: Knit 3, *mark the next 3 for the future fold as follows: connect a piece of contrasting colored yarn to the working yarn and knit 3, then knit 12* repeat from * to * until the end of the row before the edge stitch, knit the last 12 stitches as follows: connect a piece of contrasting colored yarn to the working yarn and knit 3, thus marking 3 stitches for the future fold, then knit 9.

Row 16: Purl all the stitches.

Row 17: Knit all the stitches.

Row 18: Purl all the stitches.

Rows 19-26: Alternate rows 17-18.

Row 27: Knit 3, *knit the next 3 together with 3 marked stitches in row 15 as follows: pick up 3 corresponding marked stitches onto an additional needle, knit the 1st stitch together with the 1st marked stitch, knit the 2nd stitch together with the 2nd marked stitch, knit the 3rd stitch together with the 3rd marked stitch, then knit 12* repeat from * to * until the end of the row before the edge stitch, knit the last 12 stitches as follows: knit 3 stitches together with the 3 marked stitches as described in this row, then knit 9.

Row 28: Purl all the stitches.

Row 29: Knit 6, *mark the next 3 for the future fold as follows: connect a piece of contrasting colored yarn to the working yarn and knit 3, then knit 12* repeat from * to * until the end of the row before the edge stitch, knit the last 9 stitches as follows: connect a piece of contrasting colored yarn to the working yarn and knit 3, thus marking 3 stitches for the future fold, then knit 6.

Row 30: Purl all the stitches.

Row 31: Knit all the stitches.

Row 32: Purl all the stitches.

Rows 33-40: Alternate rows 31-32.

Row 41: Knit 6, *knit 3 together with 3 marked stitches in row 29 as follows: pick up 3 corresponding marked stitches onto an additional needle, knit the 1st stitch together with the 1st marked stitch, knit the 2nd stitch together with the 2nd marked stitch, knit the 3rd stitch together with the 3rd marked stitch, then knit 12* repeat from * to * until the end of the row before the edge stitch, knit the last 9 stitches as follows: knit 3 stitches together with 3 marked stitches as described in this row, then knit 6.

Row 42: Purl all the stitches.

Row 43: Knit 9, *mark the next 3 for the future fold as follows: connect a piece of contrasting colored yarn to the working yarn and knit 3, then knit 12* repeat from * to * until the end of the row before the edge stitch, knit the last 6 stitches as follows: connect a piece of contrasting colored yarn to the working yarn and knit 3, thus marking 3 stitches for the future fold, then knit 3.

Row 44: Purl all the stitches.

Row 45: Knit all the stitches.

Row 46: Purl all the stitches.

Rows 47-54: Alternate rows 45-46.

Row 55: Knit 9, *knit 3 together with 3 marked stitches in row 43 as follows: pick up 3 corresponding marked stitches onto an additional needle, knit the 1st stitch together with the 1st marked stitch, knit the 2nd stitch together with the 2nd marked stitch, knit the 3rd stitch together with the 3rd marked stitch, then knit 12* repeat from * to * until the end of the row before the edge stitch, knit the last 6 stitches as follows: knit 3 stitches together with the 3 marked stitches as described in this row, then knit 3.

Row 56: Purl all the stitches.

Row 57: Knit 12, *mark the next 3 for the future fold as follows: connect a piece of contrasting colored yarn to the working yarn and knit 3, then knit 12* repeat from * to * until the end of the row before the edge stitch, knit the last 3 as follows: connect a piece of contrasting colored yarn to the working yarn and knit 3.

Row 58: Purl all the stitches.

Row 59: Knit all the stitches.

Row 60: Purl all the stitches.

Rows 61-68: Alternate rows 59-60.

Row 69: Knit 12, *knit the next 3 together with 3 marked stitches in row 57 as follows: pick up 3 corresponding marked stitches onto an additional needle, knit the 1st stitch together with the 1st marked stitch, knit the 2nd stitch together with the 2nd marked stitch, knit the 3rd stitch together with the 3rd marked stitch, then knit 12* repeat from * to * until the end of the row before the edge stitch, knit the last 3 together with 3 marked stitches as described in this row.

Row 70: Purl all the stitches.

Repeat rows: 1-70.

Bind off as follows: slip the edge stitch onto the right needle, knit 1, then insert the left needle through the slipped edge stitch from left to right and pass it over the knitted stitch; *now there is 1 stitch on the right needle; knit the next 1, insert the left needle through the 1st stitch from left to right and pass it over the 2nd stitch* repeat from * to * until the end of the row.

Pattern 50

Cast on a multiple of 20, plus 2 edge stitches. Twenty-stitch repeat. Repeat rows: 1-28. The edge stitches are not included in the description below and must be added. Slip the first edge stitch; purl the last edge stitch as if to purl in knitting through the back leg as follows: insert the right needle through the stitch from back to front,

109

move the working yarn under the right needle, and pull it with the needle through the stitch. **Knit through the front leg, purl as follows:** with the working yarn in front of the stitch, wrap the working yarn forward (i.e., from yourself) around the tip of the right needle, then pull the working yarn with the needle through the stitch. The purl stitch that is worked this way sets up the knit stitch to be knitted through the front leg.

Note: For creating folds, temporary mark 4 stitches in certain rows and places as described below, connecting a piece of contrasting colored yarn to the working yarn. Remove the helping pieces of yarn after the folds are made.

Description:

Row 1: Knit 4, *mark the next 4 for the future fold as follows: connect a piece of contrasting colored yarn to the working yarn and knit 4, then knit 16* repeat from * to * until the end of the row before the edge stitch, knit the last 16 stitches as follows: knit 4, connecting a piece of contrasting colored yarn to the working yarn, thus marking 4 stitches for the future fold, then knit 12.

Row 2: Purl all the stitches.

Row 3: Knit all the stitches.

Row 4: Purl all the stitches.

Row 5: Knit all the stitches.

Row 6: Purl all the stitches.

Row 7: Knit all the stitches.

Row 8: Purl all the stitches.

Row 9: Knit all the stitches.

Row 10: Purl all the stitches.

Row 11: Knit 4, *knit the next 4 together with the 4 marked stitches in row 1 as follows: pick up onto an additional needle these 4 marked stitches, then knit the 1st stitch together with the 1st marked stitch, knit the 2nd stitch together with the 2nd marked stitch, knit the 3rd stitch together with the 3rd marked stitch, knit the 4th stitch together with the 4th marked stitch, then knit 16* repeat from * to * until the end of the row before the edge stitch, the last 16 stitches, knit 4 together with 4 marked stitches as described above, then knit 12.

Row 12: Purl all the stitches.

Row 13: Knit all the stitches.

Row 14: Purl all the stitches.

Row 15: Knit 12, *mark the next 4 for the future fold as follows: connect a piece of contrasting colored yarn to the working yarn and knit 4, knit 16* repeat from * to * until the end of the row before the edge stitch, knit the last 8 stitches as follows: connect a piece of contrasting colored yarn to the working yarn and knit 4, thus marking 4 stitches for the future fold, then knit the last 4.

Row 16: Purl all the stitches.

Row 17: Knit all the stitches.

Row 18: Purl all the stitches.

Row 19: Knit all the stitches.

Row 20: Purl all the stitches.

Row 21: Knit all the stitches.

Row 22: Purl all the stitches.

Row 23: Knit all the stitches.

Row 24: Purl all the stitches.

Row 25: Knit 12, *knit 4 together with the 4 marked stitches in row 15 as described in row 11, then knit 16* repeat from * to * before the edge stitch, the last 8 stitches, knit 4 together with 4 marked stitches in row 15 as described in row 11, then knit the last 4.

Row 26: Purl all the stitches.

Row 27: Knit all the stitches.

Row 28: Purl all the stitches.

Repeat rows: 1-28.

Bind off as follows: slip the edge stitch onto the right needle, knit 1, then pass the edge stitch over the knitted stitch; *now there is 1 stitch on the right needle; knit the next 1, insert the left needle through the 1st stitch from left to right and pass it over the 2nd stitch* repeat from * to * until the end of the row.

About the Author

Internationally recognized hand knitwear designer Marina Molo has taught various hand knitting aspects over the past 30 years. In her book, 50 Shades of Stitches Vol 2, Marina Molo brings to life, in print, the most popular knitting patterns, Classic & Contemporary, for all those who want to explore designing their knitwear.

Visit the author's online store for unique items with knit prints, including tank tops, leggings, tote bags, iPhone cases, passport holders, luggage tags, wrapping paper, ribbons, pattern folders & much more at https://www.zazzle.com/store/shades_of_stitches or scan the QR code below.

Marina Molo is currently working on several new publishing projects with SCR Media Inc.

Sign up to be notified when the next release is available at **www.MarinaMolo.com**

What Do You Think of *50 Shades of Stitches*?

First of all, thank you for purchasing this book 50 Shades of Stitches Volume 2.

I know you could have picked any other books to read, but you chose this book, and for that, I am incredibly grateful. I hope that it adds value and quality to your everyday life. If so, it would be nice if you could share this book with your friends and family by posting it on **Facebook** and **Twitter**.

If you like this book, I'd like to hear from you and hope that you could take some time to post a review on Amazon. Your feedback and support will help the author to improve her writing craft for future projects and make this book even better. Just type this link into your web browser Getbook.at/Vol2 or scan the code below

I want you, the reader, to know that your review is critical and so, if you'd like to leave a review, all you have to do is copy it into your web browser **Getbook.at/Vol2**

I wish you all the best in your future success!

www.ingramcontent.com/pod-product-compliance
Lightning Source LLC
Chambersburg PA
CBHW081459070526
44586CB00019B/2423